THE CRIMINAL CASE OF JUANA AGUILAR

THE CRIMINAL CASE OF JUANA AGUILAR

Adjudicating Gender in Colonial Central America

Sylvia Sellers-García

The Pennsylvania State University Press
University Park, Pennsylvania

Frontispiece Allegory of Justice, late eighteenth-century engraving.

Library of Congress Cataloging-in-Publication Data

Names: Sellers-García, Sylvia, author.
Title: The criminal case of Juana Aguilar : adjudicating gender in colonial Central America / Sylvia Sellers-García.
Other titles: Latin American originals.
Description: University Park, Pennsylvania : The Pennsylvania State University Press, [2025] | Series: Latin American originals | Includes bibliographical references and index.
Summary: "Presents the translated criminal case of Juana Aguilar, an Indigenous intersex person tried between 1790 and 1803 in San Salvador and Guatemala City. The volume offers insight into the legal and medical systems that sought to define Aguilar's identity, illuminating intersections of gender, sexuality, and colonial authority in this period"—Provided by publisher.
Identifiers: LCCN 2025026222 | ISBN 9780271100340 (paperback)
Subjects: LCSH: Aguilar, Juana, approximately 1762-—Trials, litigation, etc. | Trials (Sex crimes)—Guatemala. | Trials (Sodomy)—Guatemala. | Intersex people—Legal status, laws, etc.—Central America—History—18th century—Sources. | Intersex people—Legal status, laws, etc.—Central America—History—19th century—Sources. | Intersex people—Central America—Identity—History—18th century—Sources. | Intersex people—Central America—Identity—History—19th century—Sources. | Intersex people—Medical examinations—Central America—History—18th century—Sources. | Intersex people—Medical examinations—Central America—History—19th century—Sources. | LCGFT: Primary sources.
Classification: LCC KGD135.A38 S45 2025 | DDC 345.7281/02536—dc23/eng/20250625
LC record available at https://lccn.loc.gov/2025026222

Printed in the United States of America
Published by The Pennsylvania State University Press, University Park, PA 16802–1003

The Pennsylvania State University Press is a member of the Association of University Presses.

It is the policy of The Pennsylvania State University Press to use acid-free paper. Publications on uncoated stock satisfy the minimum requirements of American National Standard for Information Sciences—Permanence of Paper for Printed Library Material, ANSI Z39.48–1992.

CONTENTS

FOREWORD

Latin American Originals (LAO) is a series of primary-source texts on colonial Latin America, packaged for both scholarly and classroom use. Drawn from seven languages, most are translated into English for the first time. The contributors to this multidisciplinary series are anthropologists, historians, geographers, and scholars of literature, focusing on topics from northern Mexico to southern Chile, from the 1490s to the turn of the nineteenth century.

Almost half of its twenty volumes illuminate aspects of the Spanish invasions in the Americas during the long century of 1494–1614. An emphasis on Indigenous experiences and perspectives is a series theme. *Of Cannibals and Kings* presents the earliest written attempts to describe Indigenous cultures. *The Native Conquistador* tells of the (in)famous 1519–24 Spanish conquest expeditions into Mexico and Guatemala from the startlingly different viewpoint of a royal Indigenous dynasty. *Invading Guatemala* and *Contesting Conquest in Mexico* both reveal how reading multiple Indigenous and Spanish accounts can explode established conquest narratives. We also gain new understandings of the conquest era through insight into lesser-known campaigns. These include fraught ones into what Spaniards called New Granada (*Invading Colombia*) and the Río de la Plata region (*The Improbable Conquest*), as well as efforts by other Europeans to invade places already claimed by Spain—such as the German efforts explored in *Violent First Contact in Venezuela* and the Dutch expedition detailed in *To the Shores of Chile*.

Another group of volumes explores aspects of the aftermath of the invasion era. *The History of the New World* contains the first English translation since 1847 of part of a 1565 Italian account offering an imaginative and often sympathetic view of Indigenous history in the conquest and early colonial decades. A sympathetic view of a different kind is presented through the first theatrical examination of the conquest published in Spain (*The Conquest on Trial*), providing a contrast to *Defending the Conquest*, in which a veteran conquistador vents a spirited, ill-humored, and polemic apologia for Spanish conquests.

The latter also pairs well with *To Heaven or to Hell*, in which fray Bartolomé de Las Casas outrages Spanish colonists by suggesting that they need to be spiritually conquered more than Indigenous peoples do. That volume is one in a group offering new perspectives on efforts to implant Christianity in the Americas. *Forgotten Franciscans* sheds light on the conflictive cultural world of the Inquisition in sixteenth-century Mexico. A political and religious revolutionary is burned at the stake by the Mexican Inquisition in *An Irish Rebel in New Spain*. *Gods of the Andes* presents one Jesuit's view on how Inca religion prepared Andeans for the arrival of the new faith. *Translated Christianities* reveals how religious texts in Nahuatl and Yucatec Maya reflected the development of local Christianities. And the continuities and transformations of life in Christianized Nahua families are uncovered in *Indigenous Life After the Conquest*.

One thread running through the series—sin and salvation—meets another—science and medicine—in three volumes taking us through late-colonial times. *Pandemic in Potosí* unpacks a 1719 account of the great plague that devastated that famous mining city. *Baptism Through Incision* deploys an eye-opening 1786 Guatemalan treatise on performing cesareans on dying pregnant women to explore series themes of empire, salvation, the female body, and knowledge as a New World battleground. The same concerns, time, and place are the focus of the present volume. With the subtitle *Adjudicating Gender in Colonial Central America*, Sylvia Sellers-García deftly contextualizes her translation of the 1792–1803 criminal case records of a gender-identity scandal. Her exploration of how the body of a Guatemalan who seems to be a hermaphrodite became a battleground—where popular belief and medical tradition clashed—makes for a compelling new contribution to the series.

—Matthew Restall

ACKNOWLEDGMENTS

This translation was written for students, because of students, and with help from students. I am deeply grateful to the students who have inspired, challenged, educated, and accompanied me in the process of writing this book. MC Claverie, thank you for the passion that you brought to this topic; I would not have undertaken this translation if you had not expressed such curiosity in the story of Juana Aguilar. I learned so much from your thesis and from our many conversations together about this case. Andres Grande, your paleography skills are unmatched! Thank you so much for the care and tremendous skill that you brought to the work of checking my transcription. Many other students at Boston College have, over the years, sharpened and broadened my thinking about secular and ecclesiastical criminal cases. Thanks especially to Neal Bold, Meg Day, Liam Gloster, Kate Kemp, Paige Nixon, Valentina Ochoa Saldarriaga, and Sam Ouellete, who, in the last year while I was working on this case, helped me think differently about this material.

The Archivo General de Centroamérica, where the criminal case of Juana Aguilar is housed, is an incredible collection, and I am so grateful to the archivists who have continued to keep the archive going through challenging times. In particular, I will always be grateful to the late Jorge Castellanos for his generosity, his vast knowledge, and his good humor.

I am very grateful to Matthew Restall for responding with such enthusiasm to this project and for supporting its development in the Latin American Originals series. Ellie Goodman offered wise counsel, patient guidance, and unstinting support for the subject matter of this volume. Maddie Caso made the complicated logistics seem almost easy. Thank you to Alex Ramos, Jennifer Norton, Laura Reed-Morrisson, and everyone at Penn State University Press who contributed to the making of this book.

Thank you to Erin Greb for creating a wonderful map of Aguilar's route.

I am indebted to the colleagues who have taken an interest in this project, supported the many endeavors undertaken to complete it, and recommended approaches or readings. My thanks to Brianna Leavitt-Alcántara, Dana Leibsohn, Brinton Lykes, Martin Summers, Julian Bourg, Penny Ismay, Prasannan Parthasarathi, Wendy Kline, Wan Tang, and Allison Adair. Katrina Olds, thank you for creating pockets of time dedicated to writing; I finished important revisions thanks to you. Samuel Truett took on a committee role that made it possible for me to finish this manuscript in time for a deadline—thank you! Donna Pierce offered essential expertise on the inventories of Juana Aguilar, and several of these items only came into focus thanks to her expert eye. I am deeply grateful to colleagues who read portions of the manuscript or all of it. Ana Díaz Burgos, Jeffrey Erbig, and Paul Ramírez: thank you for the encouragement, vital corrections, and excellent recommendations for revisions. Thanks to Ana's kind invitation, I presented part of this work at Oberlin College, and the feedback of students and faculty there was tremendously helpful. Thank you in particular to Cecily Miles for following up with me about a few key points. I am especially grateful to the anonymous readers for their considered comments and to Asa Ackerly, Rachel Nolan, Bill Taylor, and Kirsten Weld for offering feedback on the entire manuscript. Each of you offered suggestions and considerations that made this book better.

Boston College has supported this project in many ways. A research grant allowed me to return to the AGCA to check my transcription against the original case, and amazing librarians—including Anne Kenny and Erin Scheopner—made the fundamentals of research possible. My thanks to Dean Greg Kalscheur for approving funds that assisted with publication.

I am grateful to my family for supporting this project with interest and enthusiasm. Thank you to Oliver, Tom, Alton, and Rowan. I am especially grateful to Rowan for expressing with such certainty his convictions about right and wrong; these convictions helped me clarify my own. My parents, Martha Julia García Sellers and Stephen Sellers, somehow manage to become genuinely interested in every piece of writing I send their way. I don't know how you do it! Thank you for reading this manuscript carefully, for offering questions and suggestions, and for reflecting on idiom and translation puzzles. Thank you, Papá, for going with me to the archive in Zone 1 to help comb through documents and photograph pages. I will always remember those trips fondly.

Introduction

Overview

"I was ordered to be examined by him and was determined to (~~have the appearance~~) have parts that were more male than female in accordance with the stature of my body, a defect which, it seems to me, is not my fault."[1] Juana Aguilar, accused of cross-dressing and conducting illicit relationships with women, offered this defense during a 1792 criminal trial in San Salvador. The statement advances a disarmingly simple claim that the prosecution could not adequately counter: *I am not to blame for my body*. Indeed, although it took more than a decade and much wordier deliberations, authorities in Guatemala City's high court ended up reaching the same conclusion in 1803. They were so perplexed by Aguilar's body that they deemed it an aberration of nature, but they were also unable to find Aguilar responsible for this aberration.

In many ways, Aguilar's simple sentence is a summary of the criminal case that ensued. *I was ordered*. Aguilar did not choose to undergo such scrutiny. It was ordered repeatedly by officials. Aguilar appears to have lived for many years without the intrusion of state authorities: born around 1762 in a rural part of San Salvador, Aguilar relocated twice to larger towns before a few relationships with women in early adulthood prompted officials to intervene. Only then, beginning in 1790, were Aguilar's relationships and body subjected

1. Guatemala, "Criminal Case Against Juana Aguilar."

to investigation, launching a criminal case that included two escapes, three trials in San Salvador and Guatemala, multiple medical examinations, and prolonged periods of incarceration before an acquittal in 1803. Intimate same-sex relationships were criminal in colonial Central America, as they were in the rest of the Spanish empire. But the relationship was only criminal in this way if Aguilar was construed as a woman. If Aguilar was a man, then the crime would be different—a matter of having sex out of wedlock. And while having sex out of wedlock was prosecutable, it was a relatively minor crime in a patriarchal society that accorded men far greater sexual liberties than women. So which crime was being committed? Was Aguilar male or female? For a society that mapped gender directly onto sex, this was a vital and potentially simple question. What did Aguilar's body reveal?

I was ordered to be examined. The women who had relationships with Aguilar described Aguilar as manlike, and so authorities asked doctors and midwives to conduct a physical examination that would determine Aguilar's sex. What Aguilar says these experts "determined" is also telling, for the crossed-out statement "~~have the appearance~~" aptly reflects the confusion experienced by medical practitioners and court officials alike. Aguilar was found to have some anatomical features of a man and some anatomical features of a woman. Was this mere "appearance"? In other words, did Aguilar "appear" to be one thing while *really* being another? Or was it, as the sentence amends, not just about appearances? Was it the case that Aguilar was *actually* both a man and a woman? Or a man with some womanly parts? Or something else?

If Aguilar were alive today, it is likely Aguilar would be labeled "intersex," a term used for people born with sex characteristics "that do not fit typical binary notions of male or female bodies."[2] In the late eighteenth century, the term most commonly used to describe someone who had both male and female anatomical features was

2. Office of the High Commissioner of Human Rights, "Intersex People." As the OHCHR documents, it is estimated that up to 1.7 percent of the population is born with intersex traits. While the term is accepted by many, it also has detractors, and it is worth acknowledging that the term—any term—in many ways continues the Enlightenment-era approach of labeling difference. For other terms, see Reis, *Bodies in Doubt*. For a readable (but rigorous) study of the intersex category, see Fausto-Sterling, *Sexing the Body*.

"hermaphrodite." (Today, intersex activists consider this term a slur rather than simply outdated.) The term had been in existence for centuries; it had been elaborated by legal philosophers and medical practitioners in ways that validated its usage. But the designation was rare and it did not signal acceptance; for people in the late eighteenth century, it carried suggestions of abnormality and even monstrosity. There was no acceptable status in colonial Spanish America for those who did not neatly fit constructions of "male" or "female."

Aguilar never used the term "hermaphrodite." Aguilar also never used a male or female pronoun in self-description, since the Spanish first-person allows one (as in English) to speak of "I" and "me" without designating a gender. Aguilar did use the word "daughter" when responding to a formulaic question about parentage, but in at least one instance Aguilar's name is given as "Juan Aguilar": a masculine, rather than feminine, name. This leaves open the question of how Aguilar chose to express gender through language. As a result, I have elected not to use pronouns for Aguilar in this introduction, though it results in occasional infelicitous phrasings. Using the plural third-person is common in our own time, but in Aguilar's sphere there was no such convention, and employing "they" here risks imposing yet another unsolicited category onto Aguilar or implying that Aguilar is ineligible to use "he" or "she."[3] Spanish authorities, for their part, consistently identify Aguilar as *ella* (she), a choice that seems simultaneously unconsidered (they *saw* Aguilar as female) and conveniently restrictive. It is perhaps helpful to acknowledge the tremendous power of both Spanish and English to impose, at a linguistic level, a constrictive gender binary.

Indeed, Aguilar's choices of representation were restricted in multiple ways. On the one hand, it is remarkable that Aguilar's words survived at all; the testimony in the case feels vital because it seems as though we are hearing directly from Aguilar. On the other hand, the testimony reaches us through layers of constraint and distortion—mediated through the writing of the scribe, constrained by physical incarceration, pressured by the fear of punishment—and as a result it also feels unreliable. Surely if Aguilar had wished to present a record of past experiences for posterity, the chosen method

3. I am indebted to the anonymous reader for pointing out the first risk and to Cecily Miles for pointing out the second.

would not have been through the criminal trial that cast Aguilar as a villain and deviant, a person to be either castigated or pitied. Not only does the testimony of others—by turns vindictive, suspicious, or hapless—shape how Aguilar is presented on the page but the entire framing of a criminal case elevates the authority of officials and "experts," suggesting that judges, medical witnesses, and court scribes are the ones whose knowledge about the world really matters. By design, the ritualized protocols of the case powerfully characterize the actions of these experts as rational and normal when they may, in fact, be violent and dehumanizing.

This is true of all criminal cases, not just Aguilar's. Broadly speaking, criminal cases are attractive because they seem to channel the voices of suspects and witnesses. But criminal cases are also flawed, because they present ordinary people—people who had long, vibrant lives outside the court—through the brushstrokes of court officials and the suspect frame of transgression. When we read a criminal case, we are catching the accused person at a low point, sometimes at the most stressful and painful moment of their life, in ways they probably would never wish to be remembered. And while this would probably be true regardless of the privilege of the accused, marginalized voices are even more likely to be distorted in court documents. In Aguilar's case, as in other cases where enslaved people and Indigenous subjects were on trial, the court doubted Aguilar's very humanity. What chance does a person have of being depicted truthfully—or fairly—by a court that concludes the person is not really human?

Ethical Quandaries

I came across the criminal case of Juana Aguilar in 2012 at the Archivo General de Centroamérica in Guatemala City while researching other examples of criminality and policing in the late eighteenth century. I had read Martha Few's article from 2007 analyzing the published report by Dr. Narciso Esparragosa, which for a long time was considered the only extant source about the case.[4] At the time, as I documented the court proceedings out of general interest and a sense of recognition, I didn't realize that the case had been

4. Few, "'That Monster of Nature.'"

out of scholarly view for decades.[5] But I understood that the proceedings offered a counterpoint to Esparragosa's published report, and that in itself seemed worthwhile. It was galling to read about Aguilar entirely through the perspective of Esparragosa, whose breezy and erudite prose could not effectively conceal the brutality of his invasive physical examinations, his assessments of female libido, and his disdain for other medical practitioners. In this light, the criminal case seemed like an invaluable opportunity to hear from Aguilar directly and to learn more about the context of Esparragosa's intervention.

Not until I translated the case for a student, MC Claverie—who was keen on writing a senior thesis about the criminalization of sexuality in the Spanish empire—did I spend more time with the case documents. Then, aided by conversations with Claverie along the way, I gradually realized that the case was indeed an opportunity, but a vexed one. I had some experience with reading descriptions of gendered violence in other criminal cases. They had partially prepared me for how the colonial court failed to recognize particular forms of violence that we usually identify, including rape and domestic abuse. I found the unrecognized violence in Juana Aguilar's case analogous but distinct; where domestic violence was generally construed by court officials as a form of acceptable discipline that could, nevertheless, sometimes be carried to criminal excess, the violence in Aguilar's case was presented in the guise of routine medical examination, with no outer limit defined as unacceptable.

Repeatedly, over the course of several criminal trials in San Salvador and Guatemala, Aguilar was subjected to physical examinations, some of which sought to induce sexual stimulation, and all of which were conducted while Aguilar was incarcerated. Further, the results of these examinations were reproduced in minute detail. The illustration that Esparragosa commissioned of Aguilar's genitals is not found in the case file, but the textual description leaves little to the imagination. For readers accustomed to detailed anatomical descriptions in medical writings, these reports might well present as clinical—albeit graphic—reports. The rhetoric of dispassionate medical description argues effectively for its own neutrality, presenting

5. See Zeb Tortorici's analysis of this archival story in Marshall and Tortorici, *Turning Archival*.

a guise of rational harmlessness.[6] But such a reading is only possible if we ignore every contextual aspect of how the medical description was produced: Aguilar's construed difference of race and gender in colonial society, marginalization due to that difference, and incarceration. The effect is only one step removed from the kind of medical photography produced in later time periods, documenting with the physician's gaze the unwilling, restrained, and medicalized subject. In other words, the description is a record of what the physician observed, but it is also a record of what the physician did to Aguilar. It is an unintentional description of violence.

What does it mean, then, to reproduce these descriptions for an even wider group of readers? What can be the justification for inviting more people to witness what was done to Aguilar, at the very least enabling a voyeuristic gaze and at the very worst reproducing that violence?

Historians of medicine, historians of disability, and scholars who focus on atrocity and trauma have raised these questions in other, similar contexts. While much of their debate specifically focuses on the use of images, the larger questions apply to text as well. On the one hand, scholars argue persuasively that failing to look closely at accounts of violence, violations, and atrocity can perpetuate ignorance—even a pernicious silence—about the horrors of the past and that we have an "ethical imperative" to attend to that violence, acting as witnesses. This ethical imperative requires us to seek accountability and truth in archival materials that document trauma.[7] On the other hand, as different scholars have pointed out, there is no guarantee that a disturbing account or image will provoke a universal emotional response—say, the righteous outrage that seeks accountability—and it may even lead to more problematic emotions, such as revulsion or inured indifference.[8] Added to all this is the thorny problem of consent. In most of the cases considered by these literatures, the photographs, depositions, and other accounts were taken either without consent or actively against the subject's will. Adria Imada's telling phrase "carceral medicine" describes a

6. This manner of viewing medical description would not be possible for me or for other scholars without the field-changing work of Michel Foucault, particularly his conception of the medical "gaze." See Foucault, *Birth of the Clinic*.

7. Caswell, "Khmer Rouge Archives."

8. Crane, "Choosing Not to Look."

"juridical-medical system that worked to incarcerate particular bodies and produce knowledge about those bodies" in nineteenth-century Hawai'i; it also aptly describes the conditions under which Aguilar was examined and tried in colonial Guatemala. As Imada then argues, using the materials produced coercively by medical experts in such a setting is problematic. "Who owns or claims photographs taken of people under duress?" she asks. "Does publishing clinical photographs from these archives only serve to reinscribe that epistemic violence?"[9] The same can be asked of textual accounts that include medical "knowledge" gathered coercively.

While the debate continues and practices vary, there are clear tendencies. First, most scholars seem to have abandoned the position, conceivable in decades past, that disturbing accounts or images should be presented primarily to provoke indignation. Response is too unpredictable, apathy is not far behind, and such use does not adequately consider the subject of the image or account. Second, and in close connection, scholars seem to agree that everything hinges on *how* representations are offered. "What is the best way to attend to violated bodies and biographies without replicating historical patterns of abuse?" Temi Odumosu asks in her probing and thoughtful article about the photograph of a crying child. "Under what conditions should this document/artifact/image be seen?"[10] Sometimes, modifying the material is called for; Odumosu experiments with blurring images, and Imada crops images that show patients without clothing or in vulnerable positions. But other approaches include "insisting on contextualization" and thinking deliberately about the responsibility of the reader/viewer.[11] Imada decides, in ways I find compelling, that she will include "problematic images in an obscured colonial history of disability and medicine for constituencies like my students, in hopes that we will craft better and more ethical practices of looking at contingent bodies going forward."[12] A vital aspect of this decision is the "obscured" part: these are histories we do not know well. Or, as Susan Crane says in her essay about the use of much more familiar Holocaust images: "And so I ask my students, with no political

9. Imada, *Archive of Skin*, 8, 29.
10. Odumosu, "Crying Child," S295.
11. Crane, "Choosing Not to Look," 310.
12. Imada, *Archive of Skin*, 31.

agenda in mind: what are you going to do with what you now know?" Crane does not accept that materials should be used purely to provoke, but if they are going to be used, there should be some kind of accountability to the seeing and knowing.[13]

Like Crane, I also have my students in mind as I think about Aguilar. In particular, I think about how MC Claverie observed that Aguilar's examinations were far more invasive in an era of emerging "modern" medicine than earlier examinations had been. And I think about the comment by another student, Valentina Ochoa Saldarriaga, who opined that Aguilar's case was necessary reading because, as she put it, "we live an age of denial." It's an observation full of potential. What are we in denial about? What aspect of our denial is challenged by the case of Juana Aguilar?

I believe the episodes of medical violence in Aguilar's case should be presented (a decision you may productively contest), in no small part because this history *is* obscure and to omit the episodes would add to the obscurity. But I agree that they require as much context as possible, and they need to be accompanied by Crane's apt question, "[W]hat are you going to do with what you now know?" For you, as a reader, what does the knowledge of these examinations require you to do?

I also believe a third condition is warranted for this introduction, and that is to adopt a deliberately postcolonial approach, framing this case as one that reveals more about colonial mechanisms, mindsets, and institutions than it does about the life and identity of the subject on trial.[14] Instead of hoping to unearth some genuine, agentive version of Juana Aguilar in this case, a version that satisfyingly challenges Esparragosa's distortions, we might instead begin by thinking of the case as a magnifying glass that allows us to scrutinize habits of thought, institutional frameworks, and philosophical contradictions that are only rarely visible. Aguilar, uniquely positioned for the task, holds the glass.

13. Crane, "Choosing Not to Look," 323.

14. I have in mind the approach articulated by Ann Stoler in her study of colonial archives, which insists on focusing the reader's attention on the construction of the colonial archive rather than its "content," though this also builds on the work of other postcolonial scholars. See Stoler, "Colonial Archives."

Mobility and *Calidad* in the Colonial Period

Juana Aguilar was born around 1762 in the province of San Salvador in the kingdom of Guatemala, a region that encompassed what is today Central America and parts of southern Mexico. By then, the region had been nominally Spanish for more than two hundred years, but the kingdom of Guatemala remained Maya in many ways. In the mid-sixteenth century, Spaniards allied with Indigenous Mexicans entered the region from the north, and after several decades of warfare and shifting alliances, they established centers of colonial administration throughout the region. These centers—in Ciudad Real, Santiago de Guatemala, San Salvador, Comayagua, and other cities—gave the Spanish crown a governing presence, but the language we often use for this period, the language of conquest, does not adequately describe how Spanish institutions enmeshed themselves with Maya realities. In the early colonial period, Spanish religious and administrative functions both imposed themselves upon and adapted to a much larger Indigenous population, a vast territory that remained unknown to Spanish officials, and local geographic conditions.

While in some ways atypical, Aguilar was in other ways a representative colonial subject of the late eighteenth century, particularly with respect to mobility and *calidad*—a colonial term for the mixed attributes of race and social status. In the first trial, Aguilar was identified as Indigenous; specifically, the scribe recorded that Aguilar was an *india mestiza* and later a *Naboría* Indian from Cacahuatique, a mountainous region of eastern San Salvador that, a century later, would become a coffee-growing zone.[15] During the colonial period, most Salvadorans made a living by farming, particularly in the production of cacao and indigo, but indigo was predominantly grown on small farms during the eighteenth-century boom, and large estates had difficulty securing labor. As Aldo Lauria-Santiago observes, "[T]he fact that growers had to resort to pressure to recruit workers indicates the autonomy of Indian communities when

15. *Naboría* referred to Indigenous people displaced from their native region and taken as laborers by Spaniards. See Matthew, *Memories of Conquest*, 114; Castellón Osegueda, "Hacienda, familia, movilidad," 49. On mobility in the region, see also Matthew, "Two Bigamists in Tehuantepec."

compared to other regions of Spanish America."[16] This autonomy made possible the kind of mobility exploited by Aguilar. As a child, Aguilar was placed as an apprentice with a woman in San Miguel, a large town some thirty miles to the south of Cacahuatique. Aguilar fled the apprenticeship around 1777, at the age of fifteen, and traveled northwest to Cojutepeque, a town of several thousand people that lay more than sixty miles away (see map 1). Like other midsize towns in the area, Cojutepeque produced sugar and indigo; more unusually, its Indigenous population was more than ten times the Spanish population in size.[17] Aguilar lived there, apparently making a life and finding companionship, until being arrested in 1792. After about ten weeks of imprisonment, Aguilar escaped and fled northwest to Guatemala City in the province of Guatemala, some 275 miles northwest, living there for a decade before being apprehended in 1801 in Santa Ana, a town in western San Salvador.[18] This time, it took Aguilar fifteen weeks to find an opportunity to escape. Aguilar traveled back to Guatemala City and was arrested there in July 1802.

Each move to a distant town or city afforded Aguilar a new start and perhaps a chance at anonymity. Aguilar's choice of trade as a peddler greatly facilitated regional mobility, providing both the opportunity for commerce and a useful justification for ongoing travel. But such mobility was not uncommon, even for people who were not fleeing colonial authorities.[19] People moved through the Central American provinces to accommodate seasonal labor demands, to find new employment, and to accompany loved ones. In the last quarter of the eighteenth century, Guatemala City's population grew by the thousands as the city rebuilt itself in a new location after a massive earthquake. Many of the new arrivals early on supplied labor for the construction of new buildings, but soon domestic labor outpaced

16. Lauria-Santiago, *Agrarian Republic*, 27. See also Wortman, *Government and Society*, 11, 75–77.

17. As Clara Pérez Fabregat details, citing Xiomara Avendaño, Cojutepeque had 108 *Españoles*, 11,354 Indigenous residents, and 3,057 *mestizos* in 1807. Pérez Fabregat, "Proceso de construcción del Estado," 51; Avendaño, "Reforma incompleta."

18. Aguilar never specifies a reason for being in Santa Ana, but the statement at the end of the case about having lived in Guatemala City "for eleven years" makes clear that Aguilar had largely resided there after leaving Cojutepeque. It is likely that Aguilar was in Santa Ana for commerce.

19. Castellón Osegueda, "Hacienda, familia, movilidad."

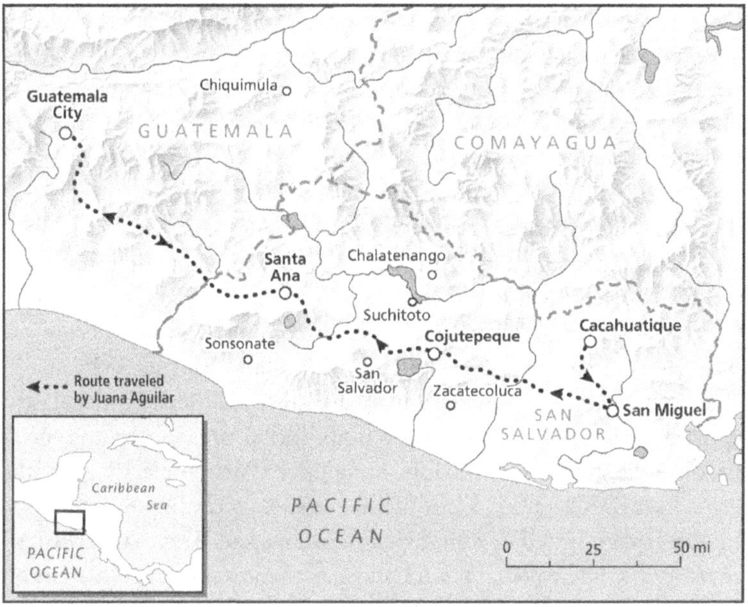

MAP 1 Route traveled by Juana Aguilar, 1777–1803. Map by Erin Greb.

construction as the principal demand, and by the end of the eighteenth century women outnumbered men by almost two to one.[20] Aguilar arrived during a period of greater population stability, when the city had already grown to about thirty thousand.

Reportedly dressed in women's clothing, Aguilar would have been an unremarkable presence among the many other peddlers and vendors who regularly sold goods in Guatemala City's central square, along the streets, and in the vestibules of larger buildings. Aguilar also would have been unexceptional as an Indigenous person in San Salvador and eventually in Guatemala. While the Indigenous population of San Salvador was growing more slowly relative to the non-Indigenous population in the late colonial period, Indians still

20. Komisaruk, *Labor and Love in Guatemala*, 9. Komisaruk cites analysis of census records by Inge Langenberg.

made up close to half of the population in San Salvador as a whole and more than half of Guatemala's population.[21]

At the same time, the designation "Indian," always to some degree fluid, was undergoing even greater transformations in the late eighteenth century. Originally devised as a legal category that would ostensibly create legal protections for "Indians," the term also identified who paid tribute and who could live in a designated Indian town. As Robert Patch explains, a growing non-Indian population that could not legally live in Indian towns resulted in complications, and "in the last third of the eighteenth century, the government began to legalize a number of towns—villas—for the non-Indians."[22] People in such towns called themselves (and were called) *ladinos*. But legal categories are not everything. Increasingly, in the late eighteenth century, people in the "hispanizing" kingdom of Guatemala, to use Catherine Komisaruk's term, identified themselves according to *calidad* in ways that omitted or minimized racial markers. Komisaruk writes that "by the late colonial period, those who moved within Guatemala's hispanized world did not always know exactly what their racial background was, nor did they seem to much care."[23] It is for that reason notable that in the early court proceedings in Cojutepeque, Aguilar identifies as *india mestiza* in one document and then as a *Naboría* Indian; the documents identify Petrona Pérez, the woman accused of illicit friendship with Aguilar, as an *India de doctrina*. This precision is in marked contrast to the frequent use by other witnesses of the word *indizuela*, a term used pejoratively to describe a woman with Indian features. Perhaps it is no coincidence that Aguilar's first flight—as a fifteen-year-old from San Miguel—was to a town with such a large Indigenous population. Afterward, Aguilar's journey through the kingdom followed a "hispanizing" trajectory: where

21. Patch, *Indians and the Political Economy*, 19–23. Patch reports, "In San Salvador in 1798, Spaniards and other non-Indians numbered 69,836 (51.21 percent) and Indians 66,515 (48.78 percent). In 1807, the total of non-Indians was 94,103 (57 percent) and the Indians were 71,175 (43 percent). The Indian presence was inexorably diminishing in what is now El Salvador." For a more detailed breakdown by city/town, see Pérez Fabregat, "Proceso de construcción del Estado," 51.

22. Patch, *Indians and the Political Economy*, 23.

23. Komisaruk, *Labor and Love in Guatemala*, 13.

Indians outnumbered non-Indians by four to one in Cojutepeque, in Santa Ana and Guatemala City they were a shrinking minority.[24]

Colonial Law and Administration

The judicial system that tried Juana Aguilar three times—in Cojutepeque, Santa Ana, and finally in Guatemala City—was in some ways old and in other ways new. Aguilar encountered more than a dozen officials, including the Indian Governor of Cojutepeque, magistrates in Santa Ana, and judges in Guatemala City. While the case seems to move seamlessly from one official to another, shuttled onward by the sure-handed signatures of deputies and scribes, in reality the case might have taken other routes; several overlapping administrative and judicial systems were in play. Exploring these systems can help us understand how Aguilar was recaptured—twice—despite fleeing across multiple jurisdictions.

Spanish America was governed at the highest level by viceroys, who were both political appointees and judicial authorities, and Guatemala lay within the viceroyalty of "New Spain," a region that stretched from what is today Panama to parts of what would become the southern United States. While the viceroy played a critical role, implementing policy and responding to the directives of both the monarch and the Council of the Indies, most of the judicial responsibilities in New Spain were performed by *audiencias*, high courts located in major regional centers—including Guatemala City—that also fulfilled legislative, executive, and administrative tasks.[25] Every *audiencia* was divided into two parts, one addressing civil cases and the other criminal cases, and it served as a court of appeal to other, lesser courts in the kingdom. As Matthew Mirow observes, the *audiencia* was a flexible body: "[R]esponding to regional events and developing in sometimes ad hoc ways, the functions and powers of

24. Santa Ana was a heavily *mestizo* city: in 1807 there were 3,479 Indigenous residents, 204 Spaniards, and 6,856 *mestizos/as*. Pérez Fabregat, "Proceso de construcción del Estado," 51.

25. For a clear and informative explanation of the viceregal judicial structure, see MacLachlan, *Criminal Justice in Eighteenth-Century Mexico*. A broader and highly readable explanation of Spanish colonial governance is provided in the research guide by Barnes, Naylor, and Polzer, "Structure of Colonial Government."

audiencias fluctuated during the colonial period."[26] The chief officials of the court were *oidores*, judges who rotated on and off the court, but a number of other officials who appear in the Aguilar case played vital roles. The *asesor*, a legal advisor to the court, usually determined which cases the high court would hear; the *fiscal*, the crown's prosecutor, could in many cases single-handedly determine the outcome of a case by offering a recommendation that the judges agreed to with alacrity. A multitude of other officials assisted with enforcement and administration. *Escribanos*, or court scribes, were responsible for both the transcription of trial proceedings and the maintenance of archival records. *Alguaciles*, comparable to bailiffs, were charged with executing the court's orders, and *alcaydes* managed the incarceration of prisoners and witnesses.

At the local level, the judiciary relied on far fewer officials. Magistrates called *alcaldes mayores* fulfilled a variety of functions, subordinate to the *audiencia* but with significant autonomy to pursue governance and law enforcement as they saw fit. Like viceroys, *alcaldes mayores* were appointed by the crown. Every town or municipality also relied on a governing body called a *cabildo*, much like a town council, which had designated magistrates, *alcaldes ordinarios*.[27] Indian communities that paid tribute to the crown, *pueblos de Indios*, had their own officials, including Indian mayors and *corregidores*, the officials charged with collecting tribute. Any of these officials—subordinates of the *audiencia*, officials of the *cabildo*, or Indian authorities—could initiate criminal inquiries, as did Marcos Perdomo, a seventy-year-old Indian Governor of Cojutepeque, when he took the initial complaint that led to Juana Aguilar's arrest. The individuals in these various systems did not always work neatly in tandem; for example, the *cabildos* often strained against the competing authority of the viceregal officials. But the existence of multiple, sometimes overlapping spheres of law enforcement provided the state with several avenues for addressing criminality.

26. The Guatemalan *audiencia* was the third created, in 1542, after the courts in Santo Domingo (1526) and Mexico (1527) were established. The fourth and final *audiencia* in New Spain was in Guadalajara (1560). See Mirow, *Latin American Law*, 23. Mirow provides an excellent and detailed analysis of the legal system and its functionaries.

27. Barnes, Naylor, and Polzer, "Structure of Colonial Government."

However, in the late eighteenth century, a bureaucratic overhaul changed some of how justice was administered in lesser courts, with results that impacted the case of Juana Aguilar. The intendancy system, a reform that was part of the Bourbon crown's effort to reassert and centralize governance in Spanish America, resulted in new titles—if not always entirely new governance. In New Spain, "the extant two hundred officials on the level of *corregidores* and *alcaldes mayores*, who were usually Creoles, were replaced by twelve intendants."[28] What had been the *alcaldía* of San Salvador, a region overseen by *alcaldes mayores*, was transformed into an intendancy in 1786, governed by Intendant José Ortiz.[29] Charged with four major areas of governance—justice, law enforcement, taxation, and defense—the intendant could not undertake the bureaucratic work for an entire region single-handedly. He relied upon *tenientes subdelegados*, or deputies, assigned to fifteen cities, towns, or villages throughout San Salvador. Cojutepeque and Santa Ana were among them.[30]

These regional deputies, like Jacobo Núñez y Araujo, who conducted the judicial proceedings against Aguilar in Cojutepeque, were nominated directly by the intendant. Potential candidates needed to meet several criteria: people who served as *alcaldes* could not be nominated; they had to be Spaniards, either by birth or by parentage; and they needed to be people of economic means and good social standing who resided in the intendancy.[31] Núñez y Araujo's repeated reliance on two "witnesses" in the case—men of high standing, almost certainly Spanish—illustrates how thin the law enforcement bureaucracy could be at the local level, even in a town of more than ten thousand. Núñez y Araujo lacked *alcaydes* and adequate detention space as well. He had to rely on private citizens for extra cell space and the storage of confiscated goods.

The situation was similar in Santa Ana, the town of comparable size where Juana Aguilar was apprehended in 1801. The deputy intendant there, Francisco Valdés, declined to pursue the case himself, instead referring it immediately to the local *cabildo* authorities. The

28. Mirow, *Latin American Law*, 25.

29. See Herrera Mena's lucid explanation of this transformation, accompanied by several maps. Herrera Mena, *Ejercicio de gobernar*, 25, 37.

30. Herrera Mena, *Ejercicio de gobernar*, 57.

31. Herrera Mena, *Ejercicio de gobernar*, 57.

magistrate for the *cabildo*, Domingo de Figueroa, took charge of the case, and while he also relied on two witnesses instead of a formal court scribe, he was able to call upon additional magistrates to apprehend and arrest other people of interest in the case. Furthermore, he seemed to grasp, in ways Núñez y Araujo had not, that the complicated case before him would likely be of interest to the *audiencia*. He took the initiative of contacting the *asesor* in Guatemala City, who responded punctually that the case did, indeed, require the attention of the highest authorities in the kingdom.

A vast collection of law enforcement agents, then, participated in the management of Aguilar's repeated arrests and trials: an Indian mayor, two deputy intendants, magistrates for the city council, and a whole host of officials at the Guatemalan high court. These officials worked together with relative ease, referring the case to other officials as needed. As Sajid Alfredo Herrera Mena writes in his study of Salvadoran governance in this period, "the intendancy system ultimately reinforced the traditionally hierarchical system of the administration of justice."[32] This hierarchy seems to have served the state well in this instance, given that Aguilar was apprehended twice after escaping. The effective transfer of the file from Cojutepeque to Santa Ana, and then from Santa Ana to Guatemala City, also illustrates the growing ability of local officials to pair law enforcement with archival management. Prior to the late eighteenth century, it would have been challenging, if not impossible, for officials to execute a case of this kind across long distances.[33] But in pursuing Aguilar, they effectively gathered documentation spanning more than twelve years, three towns or cities, and 160 miles. It is fair to say that they managed to keep a better hold of the paperwork than they did of Aguilar.

How, then, did Aguilar escape twice?

The short answer is that Aguilar was ingenious and fled from private homes rather than formal prisons. But a more thorough consideration reveals that the gendered practices of law enforcement were also to blame.

In Cojutepeque, both Juana Aguilar and Petrona Pérez, who was rumored to cohabitate with Aguilar, were jailed. Pérez was placed in the home of Vicente Rivas, one of the officials who served in the

32. Herrera Mena, *Ejercicio de gobernar*, 58. Translation mine.
33. See Sellers-García, *Distance and Documents*.

case, on September 18, 1792. On the same day, orders were given for Aguilar's belongings to be confiscated and for Aguilar to be arrested. Pérez was, as yet, not accused of any crime, but her detainment was consistent with the practice of imprisoning any witnesses who might provide evidence in a criminal case. The seizure of Aguilar's belongings, while also in accordance with the law, signaled that the crime was considered serious; for most minor crimes, including many cases involving interpersonal violence, possessions were not seized.[34] Aguilar, upon arrest, was placed in the town's jail, situated in Cojutepeque's *cabildo* building, and the Indian mayor was ordered to stand as jailer. It was in this cell that Aguilar was examined by medical experts. The day after the examinations, on September 20, Vicente Rivas testified that Petrona Pérez had escaped from his house.

The deputy intendant tersely ordered Pérez's pursuit. Several months went by, during which the proceedings against Aguilar continued. Then, on December 27, one of Cojutepeque's *alguaciles*, Simón Flamenco, reported that Aguilar had also escaped the jail. Under interrogation, Flamenco explained that Aguilar had been moved to a private home, the house of Doña Manuela Bolaño, because the cell in the *cabildo* was needed—by implication, for another prisoner. Aguilar had been placed in Bolaño's house in chains. Asking to use the facilities, Aguilar's chains were briefly removed. As soon as they were removed, Aguilar fled at a run. The episode is instructive, for it reveals once again the perceived seriousness of the crime; not every prisoner was kept in chains. Moreover, it seems quite likely that Aguilar was moved to Bolaño's house in the first place because, construed as female by the officials, Aguilar was deemed an unsuitable cellmate for a male prisoner. In Santa Ana, years later, Aguilar was also imprisoned in a private home—the house of a woman named Juliana Cateja. Significantly, the Guatemalan *asesor* had specifically instructed that Aguilar should be kept apart to avoid contact with men *and* women. But Aguilar managed to flee once again, this time by filling a rucksack with stones to simulate a sleeping figure so that the escape would not be noticed until morning.

Criminals in colonial Spanish America were always segregated by gender, resulting in different carceral situations for people treated as

34. Abad, *Pena de confiscación de bienes*, 307.

men and people treated as women, like Aguilar. For men, the *audiencia* courts and the *cabildo* had prisons of various kinds, depending on population size, that could accommodate prisoners for long periods of time. Men would be placed in prison while awaiting a trial, either as witnesses or defendants. Prior to the nineteenth century, convicted men would not spend time in prison, their punishments being served in the form of fines, corporal punishment, military service, banishment, or hard labor. (While prison time was not rendered as punishment during sentencing, it was often the case that an accused person would be released with the acknowledgment that the time spent in jail had been sufficient punishment.) Other institutions in Spanish America—such as the Inquisition—kept their own prisons, which functioned in much the same way.

For women, the only comparable institution for much of the colonial period was the *casa de recogidas,* established in both Spain and the Americas in the sixteenth century.[35] The term translates as "house of gathered women," but the English cannot adequately convey how the Spanish term *recoger* was used in colonial settings to suggest a forcible gathering that would permit easier moral instruction. *Recogidas* echoes *recogimiento,* the word used for the coerced relocation of Indigenous peoples of the Americas into new settlements, where they would be "civilized" and receive Catholic teachings.[36] Perhaps the phrase *casa de arrepentidas* (house of repentant women), which was also used to describe these houses of detainment, more accurately captures their ethos.[37] From the beginning, these houses designed to cloister women targeted their perceived sexual transgression, as many of the women placed in them were supposedly prone to delinquency, idleness, and prostitution. The explicit purpose of cloistering was to improve women's morality and, over time, to reconcile them to marriage.[38] In other words, the original purpose of the *casas de recogidas* was not to hold witnesses or defendants in pending criminal trials (as men's prisons did). It was to gather women of suspect sexual mores in one place so that they could be improved.

35. Johnston Aguilar, "De la casa de doncellas," 15. Other institutions in Europe slightly predated these. See Onetto Pavez, "Reflexiones," 188.

36. See Erbig, "Afterlives in Captivity."

37. Johnston Aguilar, "De la casa de doncellas."

38. Johnston Aguilar, "De la casa de doncellas," 16.

The first such *casa* in the Americas was created in Santo Domingo in 1526, and in the same year a home for "lost women" was created in Mexico. In these early years, separate houses in Mexico provided shelter for poor women, widows, and women going through divorce. While prisons and shelters may seem quite distinct in our own usage—one you are placed in forcibly, while the other you might seek out voluntarily—the *casas de recogidas* existed along a spectrum, with some even serving both functions at the same time. In Guatemala, a house for women was created in 1571, but not until 1715 was a *casa de recogidas* formally established in the capital. As René Johnston Aguilar recounts, the explicit purpose was to address the medical needs of sex workers, but because "there wasn't much difference between calling someone a *vagabunda* [that is, an idle or unemployed woman] and calling them a thief, between *vagabunda* and prostitute, or between prostitute and thief, because one activity led to the other and a single situation could entail the rest," the *casa de recogidas* was as much about social control as it was about medical services.[39] In a society that equated female immorality with criminal behavior, no institution that served women at the margins of society could be without carceral overtones. In Guatemala, the transition to a new capital in 1773, after a major earthquake, proved decisive for the evolution of the women's prison. At first, the forty-five women who had been held in the former capital, Santiago de Guatemala, were shuttled from one building to another (including, for a time, in a repository adjoining the gunpowder manufactory). But the absence of sufficient funds caused the *casa de recogidas* to falter, and when the institution finally rebuilt itself, it did so formally as a *cárcel de mujeres*—a women's prison.[40]

However, even after the *cárcel* lost its possibilities as a shelter, becoming a place that unambiguously held women against their will for perceived crimes, those crimes continued to be tied to sexual transgressions. René Johnston Aguilar's illuminating table of crimes (see table 1) emphasizes the degree to which women's criminality

39. Johnston Aguilar, "De la casa de doncellas," 18. Translation mine.
40. Johnston Aguilar, "De la casa de doncellas," 21.

Table 1 Causes for detainment at the Guatemala City women's prison

	Year		
Cause for detainment	**1765**	**1799**	**1800**
Homicide	2		
Aggression	5	2	
Theft with force	4	17	1
Theft			
Making of illegal alcohol	2		3
Drunkenness	4	12	5
Unwillingness to testify	2		
Indigenous women unwilling to work	2	2	
Gambling	1	2	2
Sexual crimes	26	63	46
Awaiting divorce		24	
Total	48	122	57

Adapted from René Johnston Aguilar, "De la casa de doncellas a la cárcel de mujeres: Sexualidad y disciplinamiento en Santiago de Guatemala durante el período colonial," *El taller de la historia* 9, no. 9 (2017): 12–27. Translation and emendations mine.

was inextricable from perceived sexual misbehavior, especially in the period of Juana Aguilar's arrest.[41]

Johnston Aguilar's analysis also indicates that women tended to receive greater punishments than men for sexual crimes (six months' seclusion for women versus no punishment for men) and that women of Black and Indigenous background were the clear majority.[42] While by the end of the eighteenth century the women's prison looked more like the men's prison than it had at any other point in the colonial period, it was still a place that concentrated primarily on perceived sexual crimes, and it was still assiduously segregated

41. Johnston Aguilar, "De la casa de doncellas," 23. Translation mine. It bears mention that "Indigenous women unwilling to work," my translation for *Indias holgazanas*, is a racialized crime. The term *holgazán* expresses laziness, idleness, or sexual looseness (when applied to women) more than unemployment, and so the perceived crime here was one of character rather than behavior. For discussion of how this crime was racialized, see Sellers-García, "Walking While Indian."

42. Johnston Aguilar, "De la casa de doncellas," 24.

by gender. In other towns and municipalities, the practice of separating men and women was also carefully observed, and so in places like Cojutepeque and Santa Ana that had no dedicated women's jail, escape became more possible.[43]

Policing Sexuality and Gender Disorder

Juana Aguilar's case occurred during a period of intensified policing in the kingdom of Guatemala and in Spanish America more broadly. In response to what officials characterized as a wave of criminality, police forces in urban areas expanded, and arrests for crimes of disorder that impeded productivity—drunkenness, gambling, brawling, and other minor crimes—and had been largely ignored for much of the colonial period ballooned.[44] At first blush, Aguilar's case does not seem to be part of this trend. While the cover page of the case identifies "concubinage" as the relevant crime, the title is disingenuous. From the beginning, the accusations revolve around a "heinous sin" rumored to be taking place: same-sex intercourse, or what colonial society termed "sodomy."[45] Concubinage, the crime of having (heterosexual) sex out of wedlock, and cross-dressing remained possible crimes but clearly never occupied center stage in the proceedings, since they would have been relatively minor crimes if proven to have taken place. More importantly, both charges would have required construing Aguilar as male, which officials never did. Instead, the weight of the investigation rested on the question of whether Aguilar and Pérez were cohabiting and, by implication, having sex. This was

43. A *casa de recogidas* was not established in San Salvador until 1799, and then in the capital city. Guatemala, "Sobre establecimiento de casa de recogidas."

44. For a discussion of policing in Guatemala, see Sellers-García, *Woman on the Windowsill*, and Sellers-García, "Walking While Indian." For other regions in the Spanish empire, see Martínez Ruiz, *Policías y proscritos*; Johnson, *Problem of Order*; Voekel, "Peeing on the Palace."

45. Sodomy applied to same-sex copulation. "It also applied," Lavrin writes, "to any form of sex between man and woman, married or not, contravening the physical position accepted by the church as 'natural'" (Lavrin, *Sexuality and Marriage*, 51). Prosecutors generally distinguished between "perfect" and "imperfect" sodomy, but even here, definitions varied. For some, "perfect" required penetration, while for others, same-sex coitus of any kind qualified as "perfect." See Fernanda Molina's analysis in Molina, "Sodomy, Gender, and Identity," 142.

an ancient crime, seemingly unrelated to the Bourbon preoccupation with public disorder, and it gave urgency and momentum to the case.

Marcos Perdomo's reference to a "heinous sin" is telling, because it succinctly identifies how a secular crime could be entirely conflated with a religious transgression. Indeed, for much of the colonial period, many secular crimes—including some unrelated to sex—were inextricable from the Catholic framework that defined shared conceptions of moral harm. Spanish legal codes from the medieval period, such as the *siete partidas*, unambiguously set out sexual crimes in the language of Christian mores, establishing legal foundations for adultery and other offenses that would endure into the eighteenth century.[46] These legal codes also reflected the patriarchal conception of women as rooted in the flesh, uniquely prone to sexual vices, and inherently beset with moral weakness. In the sixteenth century, the Council of Trent gave new energy to the regulation of sexuality while preserving "the patristic and medieval dialectic of flesh and spirit as two antagonistic forces engaged in constant battle," as Asunción Lavrin explains lucidly in her classic volume on sexuality in colonial Mexico. "The prevalence of the flesh could mean eternal condemnation of the soul," and the Church offered assistance to the individual struggling to assert the will of the soul over the demands of the body.[47]

In a society shaped so indelibly by Catholic values, there could be no easy separation of secular law and ecclesiastical law, a reality underscored by the way in which some offenses—like sodomy—could be prosecuted by both secular and ecclesiastical courts. As scholars in recent years have explored at length, the Spanish Inquisition, initially established in 1487 to address the heresy of crypto-Judaism, turned its attention to sexual crimes after expanding its reach to other heresies in the mid-sixteenth century. Not all sins (such as simple fornication or adultery) could be interpreted as crimes that merited prosecution. But crimes against nature—masturbation, sodomy, and bestiality—along with violations of the sacraments, such as bigamy or solicitation by a priest in the confessional, all crossed the line and warranted inquiry.[48] And not all courts

46. Perry, "'Nefarious Sin'"; Behrend-Martínez, "Making Sense."
47. Lavrin, *Sexuality and Marriage*, 49–50.
48. Lavrin, *Sexuality and Marriage*, 50–51.

enjoyed the same prerogatives to prosecute crimes that crossed the secular-ecclesiastical line. Zeb Tortorici argues that while the Inquisition in Spain was permitted to prosecute sodomy in certain cities and municipalities, the Inquisition in New Spain "by and large did *not* have jurisdiction over the *pecado nefando*, or 'nefarious sin' of sodomy, or over the other 'sins against nature'"; rather, the Mexican tribunal (which encompassed Guatemala) "was allowed to prosecute cases of sodomy *only* when some overt heresy (like solicitation in the confessional), heretical propositions (like asserting that 'sodomy is not a sin'), or a priest were involved."[49] This confusing jurisdictional distribution—why would some tribunals have the right to prosecute sodomy but not others?—reveals a genuine ambivalence about how sin, heresy, and crime overlapped.

The crime of sodomy was particularly heinous in the eyes of early modern theologians because, along with masturbation and bestiality, it "implied the obstruction of divine purposes associated with creation." As Fernanda Molina elegantly explains, "such an interpretation rests on the fact that even though God had created all existence in complete perfection, such creation was yet unfinished. In this sense, males, created in God's own image and likeness" and capable of fulfilling the mandate to be fruitful and multiply, "became direct collaborators with creation." As a result, "any deviation from the task given by God was understood as an alteration of both the natural order created by God and the social order." Here is the explanation for why sodomy could be legitimately prosecuted in both ecclesiastical and secular courts: sodomy was both a sin against God and a crime against society, since "social order was but an extension of divine order."[50]

If, as Molina helpfully underscores, the boundaries between sin and crime were unclear, so were the boundaries between sodomy and other kinds of unproductive but less heinous sexual acts. The definition of sodomy was itself something of a moving target. Was impure touching a form of sodomy? What about anal coitus between a man and a woman? Or non-penetrative sex between two women?

49. Tortorici, *Sexuality and the Unnatural*, 11.

50. I recommend Fernanda Molina's clear analysis of this murky theological debate. Molina, "Sodomy, Gender, and Identity," 142. Also helpful are Lavenia, "Contaminating Infidels"; Berco, "Producing Patriarchy."

For some theologians, all of these acts constituted sodomy, while for others only male-male anal penetration could be construed as "perfect" sodomy. As Chad Black writes, "there was uncertainty in comprehending and classifying illicit sex between women," and this uncertainty continued in the eighteenth century.[51]

It is clear that the authorities in the case of Juana Aguilar believed sex between women might be a serious crime, because the specter of a sodomy charge hung over the entire trial, but they were never required to define sodomy or to decide whether sex between women qualified. Instead, the early testimony of María Mejía so convincingly argued for Aguilar's masculinity that the trials were compelled to focus on the more immediate question of Aguilar's identity. Mejía testified that Aguilar "showed up to woo me like any man would" (using the term *enamorar*), and in the ensuing exchange, she described Aguilar's conduct in ways that accorded entirely with male gender norms: Aguilar was insistent, making advances toward Mejía three times, and then tugged her by the arm. Mejía said she "allowed herself to be taken, albeit by force, in order to find out if the rumor was true," and she discovered that Aguilar could "consummate the act like any man."[52] The rumor, of course, was about Aguilar's ambiguous body. According to later testimony by more than one person, Aguilar further conformed to masculine norms by offering material support to women during courtship, saying they would not lack for food or clothes to wear. In all of these ways, Aguilar engaged in a "gender inversion" that visibly consternated authorities, who asked Mejía how any of this could be true, given that Aguilar was known to dress as a woman and engage in women's work—two stable indicators, implicitly, of gender.[53] The court seemed at this moment to realize that Aguilar was essentially performing both male and

51. C. Black, "Prosecuting Female-Female Sex," 124.

52. It's possible that Aguilar did use force, but it's also possible that Mejía understood the consequences of presenting herself as a willing partner. In sodomy cases, both participants were guilty of a crime. And while the secular court did not comprehend "rape" as a legal category in ways that we would recognize, they did understand willingness and unwillingness in sodomy cases. Presenting oneself as unwilling in a sodomy case could significantly lessen the penalties.

53. As a comparison, I find especially helpful Chad Black's analysis of Andrea Ayala in Bourbon Quito. Ayala inverted gender by dressing as a man, whistling (allegedly) outside her lover's home, and attempting to "take" her from that home. C. Black, "Prosecuting Female-Female Sex," 132.

female behavior—dressing and working like a woman while courting and making love like a man.[54] More than gender inversion, this was gender disorder.

While sodomy in its various forms had been consistently construed as a sin and a crime for centuries in the Spanish empire, gender disorder of the kind exhibited by Aguilar was not policed so consistently. It would be inaccurate to categorize previous eras as tolerant or accepting, but we do have telling examples of how gender transformation could be tolerated in earlier time periods where sodomy was absent. Catalina de Erauso, the so-called lieutenant nun, a Spanish transgender man who fought in the seventeenth-century wars of conquest in Chile, famously received approval from both pope and monarch to live out the rest of his life as a man, even after his birth sex was "discovered."[55] Less famously, Magdalena Muñoz, who was placed in a convent in southern Spain in 1605 by family members, developed a phallus and a beard over the course of a decade, was proclaimed a man by clergymen, and left the convent reconciled to a new sex. His father was delighted because he had no other heirs.[56]

These examples, isolated as they are, would have been less conceivable—perhaps even inconceivable—in the late eighteenth century. This is because gender disorder had by this time become almost as intolerable to legal authorities as sodomy itself. As Marta Vicente argues forcefully in her study of sex and gender in eighteenth-century Spain, eighteenth-century lawmakers were newly committed to defining bodies before the law as either male or female: "[I]f laws guaranteed the 'security of its citizens,' only bodies that were labeled male or female could be useful to society and provide for such security." Legislators therefore pursued fixed identities, designating the accused as a perfect man or a woman. In this objective, "it was not enough to eliminate an ambiguous body from the

54. For the original articulation of how gender is "performed," see Butler, *Gender Trouble*.

55. De Erauso, *Lieutenant Nun*; Rex, "Ungendering Empire."

56. Vollendorf, *Lives of Women*, 11–12. Vollendorf also writes about the better-known case of Elenx Céspedes, a nonbinary surgeon who was tried by the Inquisition for witchcraft and sentenced to service/isolation in a hospital. It is worth noting that Céspedes was a former enslaved person and made no effort to conceal that they had been sexually active, both of which likely influenced the court's perception of them.

courthouse, the body needed to perform and act in accordance with its sex."[57] So Aguilar, behaving both as a man and as a woman, vexed the authorities' efforts to clearly designate a sex and thereby determine what nature of harm had been inflicted on the "social welfare of the republic." Vicente clarifies that "it was the judge's role to determine the sex of a supposed hermaphrodite in order to re-establish the natural order of reproduction and marriage, and the rightful place of men and women in this order."[58]

The concern with Aguilar's gender disorder did not replace but rather amplified the overarching anxiety about potential sodomy, which continued to trouble legal authorities in the eighteenth century despite a "progressive separation" between crime and sin. Problematically for Bourbon lawmakers dedicated to the secularization of law, sodomy could not be neatly cordoned off as religious sin: "[I]nterfering with what God intended, going against nature, made sodomy a sin in both the religious and the civil contexts." Indeed, Vicente's explanation for this inextricability reveals why Aguilar's arrest, seemingly born of a centuries-long horror of sodomy, was also born of the Bourbon preoccupation with public disorder—from gambling and drinking to poor lighting and loitering—that supposedly stood in the way of productivity. "The economic waste, the seed that could not be invested in the production of a new human being, became a 'social sin' in a society that equated its wealth with the number of its productive citizens," Vicente argues. As such, sodomy was still a religious sin, but it also "jeopardized the enlightened agenda" of Adam Smith, which made clear that "a fertile nation had no room for unproductive citizens."[59]

From the moment María Mejía testified that Aguilar had consummated the act like a man, the legal authorities understood their fundamental purpose, which they pursued across three courts and almost twelve years. Could Aguilar consummate the act like a man? Or, as reflected by the choice of dress and work, was Aguilar a woman? This became the central, vital question, and in the eyes of the court it could only be answered by medical experts.

57. Vicente, *Debating Sex and Gender*, 102.
58. Vicente, *Debating Sex and Gender*, 109.
59. Vicente, *Debating Sex and Gender*, 126.

Medical Practice and Enlightenment Expertise

In the course of Juana Aguilar's trials, examinations were conducted by at least eleven medical practitioners. First, Aguilar references one midwife and two unnamed doctors who had conducted examinations in a past investigation. Then, in Cojutepeque in September 1792, midwife Michaela Rivas examined Aguilar at the behest of the deputy intendant, Núñez y Araujo. In December of the same year, Tomasa de la Cruz (midwife) and Santiago Rosales (*maestro*) examined Aguilar again. In Santa Ana in 1801, Aguilar was examined by Juana Matías Morán (midwife), Don Sebastián Carranza (surgeon), and Don Joaquín Ciliezar (professor of medicine). Finally, in 1802 in Guatemala City, Aguilar was examined by surgeons Don José María Guerra and Don Narciso Esparragosa.

These practitioners, while all engaged in examining Aguilar's body for the purposes of the criminal case, evinced different attitudes and approaches toward the task and toward Aguilar as a person. Some descriptions are brief; others are elaborate. Some are sympathetic toward Aguilar and others are dispassionate. Some admit of doubt and others do not. It is worth reading these closely to see what they reveal about the practitioners themselves. Tomasa de la Cruz and Santiago Rosales conducted the exam (as they reported) "with great care" after washing Aguilar with warm water. Midwife Juana Matías Morán, alone among all of the officials and witnesses, singled out Aguilar's nickname as a cruel moniker imposed by others. José María Guerra argued against surgical intervention, casting the events of Aguilar's life as a "misfortune" rather than a crime. And Narciso Esparragosa, who wrote disparagingly of all the other practitioners in the case (excepting Guerra), reported mildly that Aguilar was not capable of even the "slightest erection" despite all manner of examinations and touches.

In many ways, Esparragosa's grandiose assessment of Aguilar toward the end of this criminal case steals the show—if "show" can be said to encompass both the perceived significance of the case and the fame (or infamy) surrounding it. Most likely this was intentional. Esparragosa, who was professionally and socially ambitious, unafraid of public scrutiny, and dismissive of contrary opinions, did not suffer much from a restraining modesty. Born in Venezuela, he was considered by many (and himself) the guiding light of Guatemala's medical enlightenment. He served as the head surgeon of the Guatemala City hospital, where he was genuinely an innovator in fields as diverse as obstetrics and infectious disease.[60] Esparragosa also gave testimony in criminal cases frequently, sometimes offering evidence about injuries that he had treated in the hospital and in other cases consulting directly for the court on a question or subject referred to him.

While all of the other medical experts in Aguilar's case clearly offered their testimony entirely for the purpose of serving the court, Esparragosa's contribution betrays other ambitions. His testimony is essayistic, full of citations and rhetorical flourishes, and it was probably written into the legal record with an eye toward publication. (In other criminal cases, Esparragosa's testimony could be similarly self-assured without sacrificing brevity.) This is because Esparragosa had a point to prove, and Aguilar was the means by which to prove it. As a leading light of Enlightenment science, Esparragosa wished to demonstrate that the fabled "hermaphrodites" did not exist and that all of ancient and early medicine before the Enlightenment era—as he perceived it—had been wrong to say they did.

Why was it so important to prove that "hermaphrodites" did not exist?

As Esparragosa acknowledged by referring to ancient and early modern scholars, medical practitioners and philosophers of medicine had long debated the nature of people with what they saw as ambiguous sexual organs, and many believed "hermaphrodites" were rare but real "aberrations" or monstrosities of nature. Their inquiries were part of a larger study of human sexuality, which historian of medicine Helen King frames helpfully by asking, "historically, in what parts of the body has sexual identity been thought to reside?" For some thinkers, external genitalia were indeed the most important markers of sex, but for others it was the presence of a beard, or the production of semen, or the potential for menstruation. Both internal organs and human behavior complicated the use of external genitals as stable markers, leading early modern writers to debate over several centuries two questions that King identifies as vital: "'What constitutes sex?' and 'Is sex change possible?'"[61]

60. For more background on Esparragosa, see Few, *For All of Humanity*; Sellers-García, *Woman on the Windowsill*, 96.

61. King, *One-Sex Body on Trial*, 18.

As King demonstrates decisively in her study of the early modern era, no single model of sex existed in the period leading up to the late eighteenth century, when Esparragosa strove to argue against early precedent.[62] Instead, over the course of the early modern period and well into the late eighteenth century, scholars and physicians continued to debate which markers of sex mattered most and what ambiguous bodies revealed about human sexuality. As Lorraine Daston and Katherine Park explain in useful detail, the diversity of opinions coalesced around two main camps, the Hippocratic and the Aristotelian, with particular implications for the conception of hermaphroditism:

> These traditions differed in a number of important ways, and from them the early modern period inherited two contrasting models of hermaphroditism with radically different sexual, and ultimately social, implications. The oldest, associated with the Hippocratic writers and (in this respect) with Galen, viewed hermaphrodites as being truly intermediate in sex, neither male nor female, but exactly in between. According to this theory, the sex of the fetus was determined by two important oppositions: between the male and female principles in the maternal and the paternal seed and between the left and right sides of the uterus. Depending on which seed from which parent was dominant and the position of the fetus in the womb, the offspring would occupy one of a number of possible points on a sexual spectrum, ranging from unambiguously male . . . to wholly female. . . . The second model inherited by early modern writers viewed hermaphrodites not as beings of intermediate sex but as beings with doubled or redundant genitalia. . . . This model had its roots in the works of Aristotle . . . where he discussed hermaphrodites in the context of multiple births.[63]

According to Aristotle, an overabundance of "matter" produced by the mother yielded something like conjoined twins in the offspring's

62. King's book intervenes in a long debate over this topic, which is not necessary to rehearse here. The fact of this diversity of views is also supported by other recent work in the field, including Cadden, *Meanings of Sex Difference*; Daston and Park, "Hermaphrodite."

63. Daston and Park, "Hermaphrodite," 420–21.

body that manifested as redundancies: an extra toe, say, or an extra set of genitals. As such, the "extra" genitals only gave the *appearance* of hermaphroditism; true hermaphroditism was not possible.[64] These two strands of thought were not always directly opposed to one another, Daston and Park note, and indeed some thinkers managed to blur the differences between them, proposing hybrid explanations.

As Few argues, this diversity of opinion continued, so that even "by the late eighteenth and early nineteenth century, medical frameworks of sexual difference were not uniform."[65] Esparragosa recognized the diversity of opinion among his contemporaries (his contempt is tacit recognition), but he did *not* recognize the similarity of his ideas to those of earlier thinkers. Referencing Georges-Louis Leclerc, the comte de Buffon (1707–1788), and the Jesuit Lorenzo Hervás y Panduro (1735–1809) as the *only* thinkers who denied the existence of the hermaphrodite, Esparragosa was unwittingly proposing an interpretation largely compatible with Aristotelian thinkers before him. But to acknowledge a longer genealogy was not in keeping with Esparragosa's larger claim. For him, the realization was new—a triumph of an enlightened age capable of recognizing the "delusion" of past writers. As such, he spun a narrative that characterized the midwives and doctors in San Salvador as credulous fools, foils to his superior and enlightened science.[66]

Esparragosa was not alone in this view. Others like him similarly believed enlightened science could reveal new truths about sex identity; if anything "new" did emerge in this period, it was more accurately the growing consensus around Esparragosa's view, not the view itself. As Vicente indicates, in the late eighteenth century, "natural monsters such as hermaphrodites became the focus of progressively greater skepticism." In 1780, she notes, the Spanish Royal Dictionary still defined "hermaphrodites" as people with two sexes, but by 1787 "it listed some 'credulous belief' that in Africa there were villages where all were hermaphrodites. This belief, as well as some interpretations of the Genesis story, which stated God created Adam and Eve as one, attached by the spine, were all 'a fable and a

64. Daston and Park, "Hermaphrodite," 421.

65. Few, "'That Monster of Nature,'" 171.

66. As the inclusion of midwives in the earlier court proceedings demonstrates, other practitioners were still largely considered credible by authorities. See Ramírez, *Enlightened Immunity*, 200, 212.

dream.'"[67] Vicente persuasively suggests that this shift had most to do with how nature was understood as more rational and organized in this period, and consequently the idea of a "natural monster" had lost its utility. Instead, aberrant people like sodomites were construed as "social or moral monsters" who had to be educated—and disciplined—out of their monstrosity.

Elizabeth Reis tracks a parallel shift in the work of eighteenth-century British author James Parsons, who devoted himself to proving that supposed "hermaphrodites" did not exist. With echoes of Esparragosa, Parsons sounds indignant that other men of science had believed such myths, and he hoped that after the publication of his treatise in 1741, only the "weak-minded" would continue in their mistake.[68] Esparragosa did not cite Parsons, whose text would surely have delighted him, and most likely he wasn't aware of the publication (in English) from sixty years earlier. But both men were clearly influenced by some of the same sources, centering their analysis around the supposed problem of an overlarge clitoris and citing, for example, the same work on female circumcision in Asiatic and African countries, where people "wisely cut or burn them off while Girls are young."[69]

Indeed, Parsons' observation about female circumcision foreshadowed a shift that Reis locates in the nineteenth century, when physicians embraced surgical interventions in order to align a person's body with one construed sex or the other. Both José María Guerra and Narciso Esparragosa floated this possibility in their assessment of Aguilar, wondering whether a surgical procedure might open up a passageway to internal (female) reproductive organs. Guerra testified unequivocally that such a procedure would be ineffective, and he further reasoned that Aguilar had already lived two-thirds of a lifetime—and so, presumably, would have little chance of reproducing. Esparragosa concurred, writing that in his reading of similar cases, where a vaginal opening was absent, there was a corresponding absence of internal reproductive organs.

Guerra and Esparragosa also agreed in their assessment that Aguilar could not really have committed the supposed crimes. But

67. Vicente, *Debating Sex and Gender*, 80–81.
68. Reis, *Bodies in Doubt*, 8.
69. Cited in Reis, *Bodies in Doubt*, 21.

their explanations for why differ in subtle ways. Guerra offered that the problem wasn't Aguilar's enlarged clitoris, which wasn't "robust" enough to have committed the crime, but the fact that Aguilar had been unable to satisfactorily "cohabit" with a man. In other words, Guerra suggested that Aguilar's body had made it impossible to successfully perform as a heterosexual woman. As such, he believed, Aguilar was more to be pitied than castigated. Esparragosa, for his part, argued that Aguilar could not have committed the crimes because Aguilar was not a man and was not a woman. Only a real woman could have committed sodomy; only a real man could have cross-dressed. Aguilar was neither. He argued, disputing the very logic ascendant in this era, "If she is neither man nor woman, it would be a violent law indeed that would falsify her identity as one of these two sexes in order to consider her a criminal and apply punishment." Instead, he wrote, Aguilar's sex was "neutral," like that of certain bees. So what was to be done? Esparragosa disdained the ancients who, in their ignorance and superstition, exiled supposed hermaphrodites to desert islands. "But we find ourselves in a century of greater enlightenment," he wrote confidently, "and we can scoff at such foolishness. And the case of Juana has had the good fortune of being judged by the wise and prudent Tribunal overseen by Your Grace."

Dress and Material Culture

It's possible that the Guatemalan *fiscal*, Diego Francisco Piloña y Ayala, did not entirely understand the implications of Esparragosa's recommendations.[70] Or it's possible, trained as he was at the University of Oviedo in Spain, that he was shaped by the sex-binary mindset described by Vicente and so could not comprehend "neutral" in the same way Esparragosa did. Perhaps the comments about bees and exile influenced Piloña in unexpected ways. Regardless, he seems to have concluded from Esparragosa's assessment that "it would be suitable to destine [Aguilar] to live among the beasts, without human contact." This verdict reveals an answer to an unspoken question,

70. For biographical information on Piloña y Ayala, see Real Academia de la Historia, "Diego Francisco Piloña y Ayala."

one that emerges in the silence between Esparragosa's declaration of "neutrality" and Piloña's statement of suitability: Can a person be not male and not female and still human? Esparragosa clearly does *not* say that being "neutral" disqualifies Aguilar as human, but Piloña seems to reason that it does. This can only derive from a conception, on Piloña's part, that being categorizable as male or female was a condition of humanness. And yet banishment was impractical, he realized, not to mention harsh. Instead, he proposed, there had to be a way to address the risk of what he saw as recidivism and the further risks posed by the fact that Aguilar "dressed like a woman," that is, presented as a woman while not being a woman—not being human—at all.

Aguilar did dress as a woman. Thanks to the abrupt seizure of Aguilar's personal belongings (and, later, peddler's wares), we have a surprisingly detailed inventory of what Aguilar wore and owned. According to art historian Donna Pierce, none of the items in Aguilar's inventories is unusual for a person of a rural, Indigenous background, and yet the items still tell us a great deal.[71] To begin with, the women's clothes Aguilar chose to wear indicate a specific racial positioning in colonial San Salvador. As Rebecca Earle argues, people in Spanish America were "very attuned to the nuances of dress," because clothing was understood as a racial marker; indeed, she writes, "the colonial archive is full of complaints about individuals who changed their clothing or living habits, and thereby 'became' a different race."[72] Where other people who identified as *Naboría* Indians in San Salvador might have chosen traditional Indigenous dress, including the *huipil*, Aguilar instead wore *mestiza* clothing—gauze petticoats, silk taffeta, and skirts of *indianilla*, a printed cotton manufactured in Europe in imitation of chintz from India.[73]

The inventory also signals how Aguilar was positioned in a larger network of commerce and exchange. Some items, like the *indianilla*,

71. I am very grateful to Donna Pierce for examining these inventories and for clarifying the significance of several items that I found difficult to place. For a discussion of similar items from this time period and an illuminating analysis of such an inventory, see Pierce, "Unpacking a Colonial Bride."

72. Earle, "Race, Clothing and Identity," 332.

73. Elena Phipps includes images of samples in her discussion of this textile: Phipps, "New Textiles in a New World," 10–11. See also Skeehan, *Fabric of Empire*; Earle, "Race, Clothing and Identity"; Francois, "Cloth and Silver"; Pierce, "Popular and Prevalent."

were imports that connected Cojutepeque to markets across the Atlantic, but most were local items: local thread, cheese, soap, and *rapadura*, or unprocessed sugar. Aguilar testified that some of the soap was "taken to re-sell," indicating that already in Cojutepeque Aguilar had begun to operate as a local trader. And the presence of tobacco from Copán suggests that Aguilar had valuable contacts in the black market, because by this time tobacco was considered a clandestine good, thanks to the establishment of the royal tobacco monopoly.[74] Aguilar had fourteen bundles of cigarettes and eleven handfuls of cigars—an amount that one person could conceivably burn through eventually but would more likely sell, in small amounts, to others.

The second inventory in the trial, of Aguilar's confiscated goods in Guatemala, is also revealing. After leaving Cojutepeque, Aguilar took up work as a peddler, but not as a plaza vendor—a role customarily occupied by women. Instead, Aguilar was identified as an *achín* or *achimero*, a term used to designate male peddlers, thereby suggesting that Aguilar continued to vex colonial gender categories.[75] The confiscated trunk contained some silks, gold thread, four dolls, and more than one hundred small religious tokens: rosaries, images of St. Anthony in hammered tin, and a reliquary. A few more precious items also stand out: spectacles, a pair of silver earrings, two nutmegs, and St. Ignatius beans, the last of which were most likely destined for medicinal use. These items may not have amounted to a great fortune, but neither were they of insignificant value. It bears underscoring that Aguilar, having fled prison less than a year earlier, had amassed this small stock of merchandise from nothing; Aguilar had escaped Santa Ana with only a set of clothes.[76] This speaks to Aguilar's resourcefulness and ingenuity, but it also demonstrates

74. Deans-Smith, "Money Plant"; Del Carpio Penagos, "Producción y comercio de tabaco."

75. *Achín* means "man" in Kakchikel. In San Salvador and Guatemala, this designated a kind of (male) peddler distinct from *plazeras*, or female "plaza merchants." See Méndez Zárate, "Ferias comerciales en Guatemala." See also Real Academia Española, "Achimero."

76. It's also possible that Aguilar, who was apparently based in Guatemala, had left these goods behind at the moment of capture in Santa Ana. If so, then this small cache was built from scrap after the flight from Cojutepeque several years earlier. Either way, the collection was acquired from nothing; the only question is how long it took.

the availability of goods and a density of commerce that would have enabled the accumulation of such a trove.

If Aguilar had been forced to start again from nothing, I have no doubt Aguilar would have accomplished it. But, as it happened, the Guatemalan *fiscal* determined that exiling Aguilar to a life among the beasts was cruel and impractical. The trunk of belongings, filled with rosaries, nutmeg, and silks, was returned to the accused on March 17, 1803, implicitly affirming that Aguilar could continue to work as a merchant in Guatemala City. Nevertheless, the release came with a warning. In a striking statement that simultaneously affirmed Aguilar's female gender designation but denied Aguilar a sex, Aguilar was cautioned not to "abuse" either of "her apparent sexes, which she should really already know she does not have"—presumably by using them in an intimate relationship. Aguilar was also ordered to formally designate a city of residence, the better to allow for surveillance. Declaring Guatemala City as the chosen place of residence, Aguilar agreed to the terms. The *alguacil* swore that he would, from then on, vigilantly monitor Aguilar's conduct. It's possible that the *alguacil* failed to do his duty, or it's possible that Aguilar successfully abstained from any behavior that could be construed as an "abuse," for after 1803 Aguilar does not appear in the criminal record again.

Principal Individuals in the Case

Persons are listed in the order in which they appear in the case.

Juana Aguilar / Juana *Larga:* Resident of Cojutepeque and later Guatemala City; the defendant in the criminal proceedings.

Don Jacobo Núñez y Araujo: The Deputy Intendant of Cojutepeque, San Salvador, who oversees all of the criminal proceedings against Aguilar in Cojutepeque.

Marcos Perdomo: The Indian Governor of Cojutepeque, who first receives a complaint about Aguilar's behavior.

Diego Josef de la Quadra: A man of high standing in Cojutepeque who serves as a witness in Aguilar's trial.

Vicente Rivas: A man of high standing in Cojutepeque who serves as a witness in Aguilar's trial.

Manuel Pérez: Resident of Cojutepeque and father of Petrona Pérez, a woman who had a long-standing relationship with Aguilar.

Petrona Pérez: Resident of Cojutepeque, involved in a long-standing relationship with Aguilar.

María Feliciana Mejía: Resident of Cojutepeque who is briefly involved with Aguilar and initiates a complaint against Aguilar.

Michaela Rivas: A midwife in the region of Cojutepeque who examines Aguilar.

Pedro Chávez: Resident of Cojutepeque who serves as Aguilar's defense counsel in the first trial.

Josefa Chapina: A woman who makes a complaint against Aguilar in 1790, prior to the current proceedings.

Mariano Balladeres, aka "Toruno": Husband of Josefa Chapina.
Santiago Rosales: A surgeon in the region of Cojutepeque who examines Aguilar.
Tomasa de la Cruz: A midwife in the region of Cojutepeque who examines Aguilar.
Simón Flamenco: The bailiff or *alguacil* of Cojutepeque, responsible for carrying out the court's directives.
Don Domingo Figueroa: The *alcalde ordinario* of Santa Ana, in San Salvador, responsible for law enforcement in the region.
Lorenzo Alvarado: A man of high standing in Santa Ana who acts as a witness in the criminal proceedings.
Juan Saturnino Álvarez: A man of high standing in Santa Ana who acts as a witness in the criminal proceedings.
Juana Matías Morán: A midwife in the region of Santa Ana who examines Aguilar.
Don Sebastián Carranza: A surgeon in the region of Santa Ana who examines Aguilar.
Don Joaquín Ciliezar: A medical professional in the region of Santa Ana who examines Aguilar.
María del Rosario Aguilar: Resident of Santa Ana who gives testimony about Aguilar's conduct (no relation).
Juana Nasara Jatero: Resident of Metapas who gives testimony about Aguilar's conduct.
Don Salvador de Coubtiño: Another *alcalde ordinario* of Santa Ana who, along with Figueroa, processes the case against Aguilar.
Don José Tomás de Zelaya: The *asesor*, or attorney and legal advisor, to the royal *audiencia* of Guatemala City.
Juliana Cateja: Resident of Santa Ana and owner of the house from which Aguilar escapes in August 1801.
Don Joaquín José Calvo: Chief *escribano*, or royal scribe, of the civil and criminal courts of Guatemala City.
Ramón Arriaza: A scribe in the criminal court of Guatemala City.
Don Juan Campos: The *alcayde*, warden or jailer, of the royal criminal court of Guatemala, who also takes possession of Aguilar's goods in 1802.
Joseph Manuel de Barroeta: The bailiff, or *alguacil mayor*, in Guatemala City, responsible for carrying out the high court's directives.

Don Narciso Esparragosa: A doctor and official of the Guatemalan Protomedicato who examines Aguilar in Guatemala City.

Don José María Guerra: A doctor and official of the Guatemalan Protomedicato who examines Aguilar in Guatemala City.

José Antonio Cordova: A doctor and official of the Guatemalan Protomedicato.

Don Diego Francisco Piloña y Ayala: The *fiscal,* or attorney for the crown, in Guatemala City who determines the verdict in the Aguilar case in 1803.

Criminal Case Against Juana Aguilar

[Cover page]
Criminal case against Juana Aguilar (alias Juana *Larga*[1]) for concubinage, in spite of her being a hermaphrodite while wearing women's clothing.

In the town of Cojutepeque, September 17, 1792: Don Jacobo Núñez y Araujo, Deputy Intendant of this region: the Indian Governor, Marcos Perdomo, has given me notice of a woman named Juana who has lived in this town for some years. By means of testimony given to him by an Indian woman of this same town, he learned of a heinous sin taking place, that is of a woman cohabiting with a person of the same female gender, the woman having solicited [the Indian woman] by different methods and lies in order to satisfy her cravings. In light of which, in order to discover the truth and punish the delinquent, it is necessary to order and I did order that a testimony be taken from the said governor regarding the first [declaration] given to him, proceeding then to take testimony from the accuser, to whom the corresponding questions will be made in order to pursue the inquiry.

1. "Larga" means "long" and it is used throughout the case to describe Aguilar. The nickname is never explained. While it is possible that the nickname is a crude reference to Aguilar's genitals, as María Elena Martínez has discussed, it seems likely in the context of the full criminal case that it refers to Aguilar's unusual height (referenced later in the proceedings). Martínez, "Archives, Bodies, and Imagination."

Inquiries will be made with as many people as possible. To this effect I, said Deputy Intendant, do order and sign before witnesses due to the absence of a scribe.

Jacobo Núnez y Araujo [Deputy Intendant]
Diego Josef de la Quadra [Witness]
Vicente Rivas [Witness]

On the same day, I, the said Deputy Intendant, in order to procure the ordered testimonies, made appear before me the Indian Governor of this town, and before the stated witnesses who are assisting me due to the absence of a scribe, I received a sworn statement from him. He gave this statement before God Our Father and a sign of the cross, and he promised to say the truth about everything known to him and asked of him. Asked about the aforementioned events and the notice that he had given to this court with regard to the woman's accusation, he said that he received at his home a complaint by a certain woman, the daughter of Manuel Pérez, against another. The woman complained of several improper things said to her by another woman, who was jealous of a woman named Juana, in the course of which it became clear that the two women were cohabiting, for which reason it was determined that the women should be detained and investigated.[2] The aforementioned daughter of Manuel Pérez, named Petrona, was arrested, and the other woman, because she was pregnant, was sent home and told to come back the following day. She[3] did in effect return the next day, and in this way informed the court with greater clarity: "Señor. I have come to tell the truth now, because my husband won't take me back at home thanks to this woman, because of my disagreement with Petrona Pérez, and I know the reason for it; it has to do with things relating to the woman Juana. And I have come to declare those reasons and to say what this woman is, and to say what it is that she does with women. She showed up to woo me like

2. In several places, including here, the testimony is unclear due to its imprecise use of pronouns. This sentence uses "she" to refer to three different people: Juana Aguilar, Petrona Pérez, and the not-yet-named María Feliciana Mejía. The most likely interpretation here is that Pérez complained about the words said by Mejía; that Mejía was jealous of Aguilar; and that the two women living together were Pérez and Aguilar.

3. Though she is not yet named here, this statement was given to the Indian Governor by María Feliciana Mejía.

any man would, which caused me great fear, and I thought it was in jest." But immediately the said woman Juana became more forceful, and taking her by the arm she pulled her over to a corner, and in order to be free of doubt the said complainant agreed to give herself to the said Juana, going so far as to have relations with her. And in so doing she saw that [Juana] had both what men have and what women have. With this explanation the man giving testimony concluded. He said that it was the truth according to the oath he had taken, that he was seventy years old, and he signed along with me and the witnesses.

Araujo
Marcos Perdomo
Diego Josef de la Quadra
Vicente Rivas

In continuance, in order to pursue the matter laid out in the original complaint, and in light of the preceding testimony, I called before me the woman cited by the deponent, and she made the following statement before me and the witnesses, which she did before God Our Father and a sign of the cross, swearing to say the truth about all that she knew and would be asked. Having been asked her name, her *estado*,[4] and for a statement of what had occurred between her and Juana *Larga* in accordance with what she had said to the governor of her town, she said: that her name was María Feliciana Mejía, that she was married to Antolín de Los Santos, and that both of them were Indians of the town. That what had occurred between her and Juana *Larga* was the following: one day during the hour of *siesta* the declarant was in her house spinning thread and the aforementioned Juana arrived asking if she wanted to be together, to which she responded "no," that she was married and knew very clearly that [Aguilar] was involved with another *indizuela*.[5] Juana

4. Mejía's interrogation begins with the standard questions asked of all deponents who are not officials. It was standard practice to ask about age, marital status, and racial designation. *Estado*, which we could take to mean "marital status," was a gendered term, the potential answers signaling perceived sexual virtue as much as they reported on marital state: *doncella* indicated an unmarried virgin; *soltera* indicated an unmarried woman who had engaged in sex before wedlock; *casada* indicated married; and *viuda* indicated widowed.

5. A derogatory expression for a woman with features construed as Indigenous.

replied that she would leave [the other woman] if [Mejía] would be with her, to which she replied the same words stated above. Upon which the stated Juana withdrew to her home, leaving the declarant in the same place where she found her spinning thread. [She said] that having continued in her advances a second and third time, [Juana] got her way on this last occasion, pulling her by the hand, even though the declarant resisted, demurring because Juana *Larga* was involved with the other *indizuela*. And so Juana offered that she would not bother her again after this occasion, by which means she succeeded in satisfying her cravings. And although afterwards on other occasions the said Juana has tried again with the declarant, she has refused, partly because of her status [as a married woman] and partly out of knowledge of the illicit friendship with the other *indizuela*. [She said] that this had occurred in the previous year of 1791 in the month of July. She was asked how and why Juana's relationship with an *indizuela* could be used as an excuse, given that this Juana was publicly known to be a woman who dressed according to her sex and engaged in women's work. She replied that it is true that she knew her to be a woman, having seen her dressed as one, but that she had heard it said that she made advances on women, and at the time she was involved with the *indizuela* who has already been mentioned. And that the declarant, having not believed the rumors, allowed herself to be taken, albeit by force, in order to find out if the rumor was true.

Asked about what she saw in the said act with the aforementioned Juana, she said that what she saw was that [Juana] could consummate the act like any man. [She said] that this was all that she could testify and that it was the truth by the oath that she had made, which she did affirm and ratify. She said that she was twenty-two years old and did not sign because she could not. I signed with the aforementioned witnesses, due to the absence of a scribe.

Araujo
Diego Josef de la Quadra
Vicente Rivas

Then I, the Deputy Intendant, in light of the previous statements, ordered Petrona Pérez to come before me and before the witnesses here named, and she swore before God Our Father and a sign of the cross, promising to tell the truth about what she knew and what she was asked. Being asked about the aforementioned events, she was exhorted to tell the truth about the said interactions between her and Juana *Larga* in the prior statement, she said: that she has had no relations of the kind described with Juana *Larga*. What happened was that María Feliciana Mejía had gone to the house of the declarant to dispute with her about certain words she had heard spoken about her from Esteban Ramírez, who had said them while aggrieved with the said Mejía. And when [Mejía] learned he had said them to her, [Mejía] had gone to fight with her, to the point where they were laying hands upon each other, and that apart from this there had been no other event resulting in discord with the stated Mejía. And although she was asked again about the event described by the Indian Governor in his statement, which appears on the second page of this case document and begins on the second line, she said that it did not happen in that way and she did not make the demand as stated. The only thing that happened was what she has already declared. And this is the truth according to the oath she has taken, which she does affirm and ratify. She said she was about eighteen years old and did not sign because she knows not how. I did so with the nominated witnesses and hereby certify.

Araujo
Diego Josef de la Quadra
Vicente Rivas

Given the preceding declaration, and in light of the denial made by Petrona Pérez about the accusations, which give some indication of being true: Place her in custody in the house of Vicente Rivas, who is charged with her care until a determination can be made. [Orders are given to] find Manuel Pérez, father of said Petrona, who shall give testimony about what occurred between his daughter and María Feliciana Mejía. At the same time, Juana *Larga* shall be taken into custody and all of her belongings shall be confiscated. This I do order and sign, Don Jacobo Núñez y Araujo, Deputy Intendant appointed to the Intendancy of this Region of Cojutepeque, 18 of September, seventeen hundred and ninety-two, before witnesses due to the absence of a scribe.

Jacobo Núñez y Araujo
Diego Josef de la Quadra
Vicente Rivas

On the same day:

Being in the company of one of the witnesses of this trial, I did hand over custody of Petrona Pérez, and he agreed to keep her and preserve her in his power until given other instructions by this court.

Araujo

Vicente Rivas

In continuance, a search was made for Manuel Pérez, and notice was given at his house that he was in his fields, which I do make note of here and sign.

Araujo

On the same day, I, the said Deputy Intendant, in light of the previous statement, went to the house where Juana *Larga* resides and in the company of the witnesses made an inventory of the belongings contained there, which I do here record:

One trunk bound in uncured leather and horsehair
A used underskirt of printed *indianilla* multicolored with no ruffles
Two handfuls of whole-leaf tobacco from Copán
Two small flasks of clear crystal = and one black one
One small box containing six crystals
One carafe made of crystal, with a stopper
One spool of thick local thread, which was said to be pawned for one *real*
Another trunk the same as the previous one, containing some very used underskirts of *indianilla*, trimmed and with ruffles of fine linen
And others with blue thread, very used, with no ruffles
And another underskirt with ruffles, very heavily used; a large kerchief of fine linen, very used, with ruffles.
A square cloth of white burlap, used, with blue stitching
A veil of black cloth with silk double taffeta, very purple, used[6]
A gauze petticoat, blue, with netting
A tablecloth of local fabric, used
A napkin of the same cloth, used

6. This would be purple due to the fading of black dye.

A piece of netting, dyed, for use with a slip
A small mirror, broken in three spots
Two lengths of ribbon of point lace of lamé, striped
Two knives for cutting cheese
Five balls of soap
Fourteen small handfuls of cigarettes made of corn husks and paper
Eleven small handfuls of cigars made of tobacco from Copán
One napkin with three pieces of cut cheese
Two bundles of solid brown sugar[7]
One tinderbox, with extinguishers
One partly eaten cheese, with about a third missing, which is estimated to weigh about sixteen pounds.

The stated Juana having said that she had no additional belongings other than those listed here, she added to them three more pieces that were in the possession of Juana Calistro that she gave her as sweets and twenty-nine given to María Ortiz for the same reason. And that she owed five pesos and four *reales* to Señora Antonia Castillo, [for] the remainder of two cheeses she had taken, and two pesos to Thomasa Mauricio for some of the soap which she had taken to resell. In the presence of Simón Reyes, the stated belongings were turned over to him to be held in his possession, all on the same terms, with the exception of the handfuls of tobacco, the cigarettes, and the cigars, which will be held separately because they are clandestine goods. He was also advised that the cheese, sugar, and soap should be dispensed with and sold. He agreed to do so and to preserve the remaining confiscated belongings in his possession until another instruction was given to him. He did not sign because he does not know how; I did so with the two nominated witnesses.
Jacobo Núñez y Araujo
Diego Josef Quadro
Vicente Rivas

Immediately I, the stated Deputy Intendant, ordered that Juana Larga be placed in one of the rooms of the *cabildo* of this town, charging

7. This is *rapadura*, boiled cane sugar that is poured into molds until it cools and solidifies, which continues to be made and sold today.

the Indian mayor, who serves in the role of *alcayde*, with her care. Which I do here affirm and sign.

Araujo

On the same day, having called Manuel Pérez, *Indio natural* of this town, before me and the nominated witnesses, I received his oath, which he made before God Our Father and a sign of the cross, promising to tell the truth about what he knew and was asked. Asked about the exchange between María Feliciana Mejía and his daughter, Petrona, and what motives there were for it, he said: that María Feliciana Mejía had come to the declarant's house seeking Petrona, daughter of the declarant, and did not find her, and a little girl had told [Feliciana] that [Petrona] was at a neighboring house, where the said Feliciana went to find her. The declarant, wanting to know why [Feliciana] was looking for his daughter, went a little while later to the house and found them both exchanging blows, and for this reason he took a stick and hit them with it, first one and then the other, by which means he ended the fight. [He said] that the motive for the fight was that Diego Beltrán had sold some sugarcane to Feliciana's husband, and since some of the cane was delivered in bad shape, they needed to discuss the particulars, and because Feliciana thought that the son of the declarant had been the one to relate this, she went to inquire. Until it got to the point where it was reported to the governor, and then it came out that the said Feliciana had not started the argument because of the sugarcane, as the declarant had thought, but because of a woman named Juana. That this is all that he knows, because the governor had told him that his daughter had confessed it to him in private, and that the declarant had, on the governor's orders, returned to his house. And that this is the truth according to the oath he has taken, that he is fifty-eight years old and did not sign because he does not know how to. I signed in the presence of the named witnesses, which I certified.

Araujo
Diego Josef de la Quadra
Vicente Rivas

In light of these documents: Proceed by making an examination of Juana *Larga*. Michaela Rivas, the midwife in this region, is named as the person who will examine her under oath and will report the truth of what she finds. This I do order and sign, Don Jacobo Núñez y Araujo, Deputy Intendant appointed to the region of Cojutepeque, on September 19, 1792, before witnesses due to the absence of a scribe.

Jacobo Núñez y Araujo
Diego Josef de la Quadra
Vicente Rivas

On the same day I had brought before me Michaela Rivas, who was informed of the previous statements in which various speculations were made about this matter, and understanding them, she did swear before God Our Lord and a sign of the cross, offering to complete punctiliously the examination asked of her. She did not sign because she did not know how. I did so before the named witnesses.

Araujo
Diego Josef de la Quadra
Vicente Rivas

Consequently, Michaela Rivas appeared before me, the said Deputy, and the named witnesses and said: that by virtue of the order given to her and the oath she had taken, she had gone to the *cabildo* of this town and found in one of the rooms there a person who appeared to be a woman. And that in accordance with her orders, she did conduct the examination as directed, and that having completed it she observed that the woman, in her natural parts, had a small male member (about as long as two fingers are wide), and that at the same time she has the parts of a woman with the corresponding opening, and that this is the truth according to the oath which she has taken, which she does affirm and ratify. She said she was sixty years old and has been a midwife for thirty-eight years. She did not sign because she does not know how; I did so along with the named witnesses, which I do certify.

Araujo
Diego Josef de la Quadra
Vicente Rivas

Cojutepeque, September 20, 1792

On this date Vicente Rivas appeared and made known to the court that the *India* Petrona Pérez had fled the night before, climbing out of the room where she had been placed in custody. In light of which the

corresponding orders were given to the Justices of the town for her apprehension, which I do make note of here and sign.
Araujo

Juana de Aguilar, known and reported to be an *India mestiza,* resident of this town, and imprisoned in the Royal Prison, does appear before Your Honor and say: That Your Honor was persuaded to imprison me for having, as it was said to me, gone about in woman's dress while making my way as a man, and that at the same time I have had sexual congress with one or two *Indias,* according to the charges against me, and these charges are invalid, for without a doubt they have emerged due to some enmity against me, and they have wanted to make me an accomplice in such a sordid and grave crime. The same thing happened in the year 1790 when Don Francisco Rodríguez was the Deputy Intendant of this region, and he ordered me incarcerated due to a complaint made by Josefa, the wife of Mariano Toruno, due to a certain grudge she had against me, all of which resulted in the governor ordering that I be examined by an *Español* and the same thing was done in the jail by a midwife. And having found no defect on my person I was set free, and similarly in the town of Sensuntepeque, where Don Manuel Ximénes was Deputy Intendant, I was ordered to be examined by him and was determined to (~~have the appearance~~) have parts that were more male than female in accordance with the stature of my body, a defect which, it seems to me, is not my fault. For which reason I do plead with Your Honor to order a thorough examination by female or male experts to demonstrate that there can be found on me nothing more than minor defects of nature. So saying, I do plead with Your Honor to do as I have asked, as it is just, and I swear not to act in this with malice. I do not know how to sign.

Add the document to the file, and in time it will be considered. I do hereby order and sign, Don Jacobo Núñez y Araujo, Deputy Intendant of this region of Cojutepeque, on September 23, 1792, before the witnesses due to the absence of a scribe.
Vale.
Jacobo Núñez y Araujo
Diego Josef de la Quadra
Vicente Rivas

I, Don Jacobo Núñez y Araujo, Deputy Intendant of this region, having seen these documents do order: make it known to Juana *Larga*, imprisoned for charges in this case, that she should name a lawyer who will undertake her defense. She should be cautioned that he shall be appointed ex officio, proceeding to make the necessary declarations before me. This I do order and sign in the town of Cojutepeque on 26 November, 1792, before witnesses due to the absence of a scribe.

Jacobo Núñez y Araujo
Vicente Rivas

By order of His Grace, I communicated the previous order to Juana *Larga*, and in recognition of it she said that she would name Pedro Chávez, of this neighborhood. She did not sign because she said she did not know how. I did so,

Vicente Rivas

I subsequently made Pedro Chávez appear before me in this court, and I made known to him that Juana *Larga* had named him as her defense, and he said that he would accept it and did accept it, and he swore before God Our Lord and a sign of the cross to defend her in this trial, and if there were circumstances beyond his knowledge he would consult with people with scientific knowledge and good conscience who would guide him toward a better defense. And I, the judge in this case, assigned him this charge and gave him the power to pursue it freely and without hindrance, and he did sign with me and the other witnesses, due to the absence of a scribe.

Araujo
Pedro Chávez

On the same day, I, the said Judge, accompanied by the witnesses assisting me, went to the building of the *cabildo* of this town and in its rooms made them produce the woman incarcerated in this trial and before the stated witnesses and in the presence of her defense she made the oath before God Our Lord, and a sign of the cross, upon which she promised to say the truth in all that she knew and would be asked, and having explained to her the gravity of the charges and the penalties, she was asked the following: she was asked her name, how old she was, what her status was, where she was from, why she fled from the custody of her parents and who they were, who arrested her and for what reason, and she replied. She said that her name is Juana Antonia de Aguilar, about thirty years old, *soltera*, calidad *Naboría*, that she is native to the town of Cacahuatique, that she is the legitimate daughter of Isinto de los Santos and of Agustina Aguilar, that these parents sent her to learn to read with Cayetana Palona in the City of San Miguel, and that she fled from her custody some fifteen years ago. That she is imprisoned due to the orders of the present judge, and that she presumes that she has been arrested because María Mejía, *India* of this town, told the Indian Governor that she was in an illicit friendship with an *india de doctrina*[8] called Petrona Pérez, claiming that [Aguilar] had forced [Mejía] to have sex, which she knows was reported to this court.

Asked what knowledge she has of María Feliciana Mejía, and [how many times] they have seen each other alone and what occurred on those occasions, she said that she has or had knowledge of this person and has communicated with her, but that she [Juana] has never spoken to her alone; and she has gone to her house but only to speak with her father and not for any other reason.

Asked why she had gone to the house of said María Feliciana Mejía at a time when the house was quiet and what words they exchanged, she said: that it is true that on one such occasion she did go to the house to leave her two sweet potatoes and [Mejía] was alone, and on that occasion they talked about certain events in the town of Tonacatepeque[9] and about some other things that had happened to her in this town, and nothing else.

Asked if after this encounter she had gone back to the house and what conversations they had she said that she had gone back on another occasion when [Mejía's] husband was there, and on no other occasion, and that time [the declarant] did not speak to her but spoke instead to her husband.

She was charged with failing to tell the truth, for the declaration of said Mejía indicates that one day during the hour of *siesta* [Mejía] was spinning, sitting in the door of her house, and [Aguilar] arrived, asking her to be in an amorous relationship with her and [Mejía]

8. A *doctrina* was a settlement created by Spaniards for the instruction and conversion of Indigenous people.

9. A town, now a municipality, in central San Salvador.

replied that for one thing [Mejía] was married and in addition [Aguilar] was in a relationship of the kind she was proposing with another *indizuela*. And in spite of this [response], she suggested it a second and third time, saying that she would let her be whenever she desired, until on one occasion she consented to the request, and they had intercourse, [Aguilar] acting as the male. She said in response that she is innocent of all that is here charged, and she refers back to what she has already said.

Asked what motive María Feliciana Mejía would have for saying that [Aguilar] was in an illicit relationship with the stated *india de doctrina*, and if at any point she has lived alone with her, she said that she presumes [Mejía] would say this because of the frequency with which [Aguilar] went to [Pérez's] house to see her mother who made her chocolate, and to whom she gave firewood, water, and other necessities, and that she has never lived with her and that is her answer.

Asked with whom she kept company when she was absent from this town last year, before going to deliver the sweet potatoes to the said Mejía, and what places she frequented, she said that it is true that last year she was in the town of Sensuntepeque, and she was living with the said María Pérez for some days until she came with her to this town and that is her answer.

Asked if she knows why the governor of Sensuntepeque had ordered that she be examined, as stated in her previous declaration, and if it coincided with the time when she was together with María Petrona Pérez, she said that when the governor of Sensuntepeque had sent her to be examined it was due to a complaint given by an *Indio* of that town—whose identity she does not know—and that it was in that same time period and that is her answer.

Asked if she knows why she was arrested in the year 1790 by the Deputy Intendant, Don Francisco Rodríguez, she said that it was because she had fought with Josefa Chapina, wife of Mariano Toruno, over some jars. [Chapina] had felt aggrieved and had gone to declare against her saying that [Aguilar] was a man, and that [Josefa] knew it because [Aguilar] had wanted to force herself upon her on one occasion so that they would have relations and as a result it was ordered that she be arrested and that is her answer.

Asked why she denied the truth in response to the question posed to her, about whether or not she lived alone with Petrona Pérez, to which she had responded "no," only to later confess that they had been together in Sensuntepeque, she said that she had denied it because she assumed that the question related to whether they had lived together in her own home, not somewhere else. With which I ordered that the confession be suspended, to be continued at a convenient time, and it was read to her in the presence of her attorney and was affirmed and ratified. She did not sign because she knew not how, and I did so in front of the witnesses due to the absence of a scribe.

Araujo
Pedro Chavez
Vicente Rivas

Subsequently I, the said Deputy Intendant, in light of the references made to Josefa Chapina of this neighborhood, and before the witnesses assisting me, did take [Josefa Chapina's] oath, which she made before God Our Lord and a sign of the cross, and charged with the gravity of this oath she promised to give the truth about all that she knew and was asked. And being asked about what she knew regarding these circumstances, she said that she has never had any disagreement with Juana *Larga*, but it is true that her husband told the former Deputy Intendant, Don Francisco Rodríguez, that the said Juana had wanted to force her to have sex with her, which her husband had said because it was true that on one occasion, when she was single, she had lived with her in a house with an *India* from this same town named Vitoria, and that the stated Juana had persuaded [Chapina] to go to the river to bathe, and ~~once they arrived~~ that once the declarant had taken her clothes off, [Aguilar] had remained sitting nearby, fully dressed, and that by and by the stated Juana had said that if she wished it, she would not lack for food and clothes to wear, to which [Josefa] asked what she wanted from her [in exchange]. But she was already drawing away from her, and she was able to pull away because some *Indios* arrived at the same place where they were. And that for this same reason she separated from her and found a place to live elsewhere. That then a few days later she heard it said in the plaza that Juana *Larga* was a man.

Asked whom she heard saying this and who else was present, she said that she could not remember who had said it, nor could she remember who else had heard it said because it was six years ago.

Asked if she knows whether [Aguilar] had done the same with other women or solicited them in some other way, she said that it is public knowledge that she has been living out of wedlock with Petrona Pérez, *India* of this town, and although other questions were made of her she replied with what has already been said, and when her declaration was read to her she said that she remembered that what was previously asked about a disagreement was true, that in fact they had fought over some jars in the plaza, for which reason her husband (who was present) went to make his complaint, and then told the Deputy Intendant the events referred to relating to a solicitation made by the said Juana *Larga*. And she knew from her that it resulted in her being imprisoned at that time. All of which she affirmed and ratified, stating that she was twenty-six years old, that she had no enmity[10] in the case and she did not sign because she knew not how; I did so in front of the witnesses due to the absence of a scribe.

Araujo
Vicente Rivas

Subsequently I ordered to appear before me in this court Mariano Balladares, alias Toruno, and before the witnesses assisting me, I did give him the oath, which he made before God Our Lord and a sign of the cross, and under penalty of this oath and reminded of its gravity and the consequences of it, he promised to tell the truth in all that he knew and was asked. And asked about the events in the previous declaration, he said that he knows Juana *Larga*, and that it is true that she had fought with his wife because his wife charged her for a certain business matter, and due to the resulting argument the declarant went to the former Deputy Intendant, Don Francisco Rodríguez, to make a complaint, and among the many reasons he gave was that no man should be among so many women.

Asked what reasons he gave to the Deputy Intendant for his claim, he said that he made the claim because of her way of expressing herself and her manners when he was in her presence, as well as

10. The phrase here is "no le tocan las generales," also sometimes written as "no le tocan las generales de la ley." This stock phrase indicates that no general objections—such as minority of age, enmity toward the accused, intimacy or kinship with the accused—can be imputed against the person testifying.

because it was public knowledge that she was a man. This motivated him to make it known to law enforcement in the terms described, and although other questions were made to him his stated replies satisfied all of them, and he affirmed and ratified the statement, declaring that he was fifty years old and had no enmity in the case. He did not sign because he knew not how; I did so before the said witnesses due to the absence of a scribe.

Araujo
Vicente Rivas

In the town of Cojutepeque on December 19, 1792, Don Jacobo Núñez y Araujo, Deputy Intendant of this region, having seen the documents in this case and in light of the blame that is imputed to Juana ~~Garcia~~ Aguilar, I do order that a confession be taken, the accused having been properly remonstrated. This I do order and sign before the stated witnesses due to the absence of a scribe, which I do certify,

Jacobo Núñez y Araujo
Diego Josef de la Quadra

On the same day and year, I, the Deputy Intendant, accompanied by the stated witnesses, did go to the royal jail in this town, where I ordered to appear before me Juana Aguilar, the prisoner in this case, in order to take her confession. In the presence of her defense, I gave her the oath, which she made before God Our Lord and a sign of the cross, on pain of which she promised to tell the truth in all that she knew and was asked. Asked about whether it was true that her name is Juana Aguilar, that she is about thirty years old, that she is a *natural* of the Pueblo of Cacahuatique, she said it was true that her name was Juan Aguilar,[11] around thirty years of age, and originated from the town of Cacahuatique, in accordance with her previous testimony given in the prior pages, which were read to her word for word, and she said she was the same person and that was her answer.

11. The "a" here is clearly missing. Whether it is a mistake or an intentional change, the name is written as "Juan Aguilar." However, the formulation in other parts of the sentence—whether they be Aguilar's words or the scribe's rendition of them—is feminine.

Charged with the fact that she had carried out with willful intent what she is accused of by María Feliciana Mejía, *india natural*, married, resident of this town, during the hour of *siesta*, she said that although she had gone to the house of Feliciana Mejía at the stated hour, she had gone to deliver some sweet potatoes, with the news that her stepmother was ill, and that she had done this with the motive of being neighborly, and that is her answer.

Asked how she can deny the truth of what is asked of her, when it is patent in the statement made by the said Feliciana, that having arrived at her house, and found her spinning at the time of the *siesta*, the declarant propositioned her, asking if she wanted to be with her, and she persisted in this scheme until on another occasion she achieved her intent. She was charged with lying and ordered to tell the truth, and she said that she refers back to what she has already declared, and everything set out by the said Mejía is false for the reasons that she has already stated, and that is her answer.

In this willful blindness, the said Juana Aguilar continued in her denials, arguing that she knew the midwife had affirmed that she had not found anything on her person that indicated she was a man. This despite the statements on the reverse side of folio 9 and the following page, where the stated midwife declares and affirms that she found in her examination of the said Juana Aguilar a male member. Let a new examination be conducted by the *Maestro* Santiago Rosales, who serves as a surgeon in this town, who will be sworn in for the purpose; and for the execution [of this examination] let there be verification by Tomasa de la Cruz, *India* of this town, who serves in the office of midwife. Let her oath also be taken, and, in the meantime, this confession will for now be suspended and reconvened when it is convenient. And the mentioned Juana said that what she had declared was the truth by the oath that she had taken, and she did not sign because she did not know how. I did so before the named witnesses, which I do certify.

Araujo

Diego Josef de la Quadra

On the same day, I, the said Deputy Intendant, in continuance of this trial, did order to appear before me the *Maestro* Santiago Rosales, who plies his trade as a surgeon, and the *India* Tomasa de la Cruz, who plies hers as a midwife, and when they were present, I familiarized them with the orders that have been given to examine and identify Juana Aguilar. Once communicated, they said they would accept and they did accept in the presence of the stated witnesses, swearing before God Our Lord and a sign of the cross, to make an examination, with all due legality and in accordance with the expertise that they have in their respective professions. And the one who knows how to sign did, and for she who could not I did so before the named witnesses, which I do certify.

Jacobo Núñez y Araujo
Joseph Santiago Rosales
Diego Josef de la Quadra

Subsequently, the *Maestro* Santiago Rosales, who plies his trade as a surgeon, and Tomasa de la Cruz, midwife of this town, appeared before me and said in my presence and in the presence of the witnesses assisting me that in light of the charge made to them for the examination of Juana Aguilar, and acknowledging the oath they had taken, they passed before me into one of the rooms of the *cabildo,* which was opened for them by the *alcalde* of this same town, Anastacio Flamenco. And finding the said Juana in the room, they had her placed on a bed, in order to conduct the stated examination, and what they both discovered was that the male member that she has is about an inch long, with very little else, but that this member has no opening whatsoever, from which to expel semen, only in the other feminine channel [is there an opening]. They made this inspection with great care, washing the bodily parts with lukewarm water. And this is the truth, in accordance with the oath that they took, which they do affirm and ratify, and having heard read back to him this declaration the first [examiner] said he was twenty-eight years old, with twelve years of experience in surgery; and the second [examiner] said she was fifty-eight years old with more than thirty years of practice. And the one who could sign did so, and for the one who could not I signed with the named witnesses, which I do certify.

Araujo.
Joseph Santiago Rosales
Diego Josef de la Quadra
Vicente Rivas

In the town of Cojutepeque, on the 27th of December of the current year, before me and the witnesses assisting me, one of the *alguaciles* of the town did appear and he said that Juana Aguilar, the prisoner in this trial, had fled the prison where she was kept, in light of which notice should be sent, and I hereby do send such notice, to the *alcaldes* and other law enforcement officers of this town in search of her, sending notice to those in other jurisdictions. This I do order and sign, I, Don Jacobo Núñez y Araujo, Deputy Intendant in this region, before the presence of witnesses due to the absence of a scribe.

Jacobo Núñez y Araujo

The warrant was sent out.

Vicente Rivas

Subsequently I took the sworn testimony of the *alguacil* who gave the prior notice, whose name is Simón Flamenco, and he formalized his statement [by taking the oath] before God Our Lord and a sign of the cross, and he promised to say the truth about what he knew and what was asked of him. And asked about what he had said previously and how he knew about the flight of Juana Aguilar, how she fled and if anyone else was present, he said that because it had been ordered by me the present judge that since the room that held her was required [for other purposes] she should be placed in chains in the house of Doña Manuela Bolaño. He did so in compliance with the command, and a notice was sent to him with a servant that when Juana had asked to be taken out in order to do her necessities, they had removed the chain, and she had fled from the common area at a run. And because the person guarding her was a woman, what she did was to go and notify the declarant. That this is what he knows, and the truth according to the oath he has given, and he ratified it and said that he was about thirty years of age and did not sign because he could not. I did so with the said witnesses.

Araujo

Vicente Rivas

Cojutepeque, May 30, 1801:[12]

12. Though the writings appear to continue without pause, there is a temporal break here. The last action taken in 1792 was the warrant sent for Aguilar. At this point, nine years later, the official takes the case up again.

Having reviewed these documents requested by the First *Señor Alcalde* in Santa Ana, [documents] which recount the case pursued against Juana *Larga* for the charge of *concubinato* with her servant, the result of which was the repeated escape of this prisoner due to the absence of a secure jail in which to keep her, I will hereby send these documents to the said *Señor Alcalde* with the goal of preventing Justice from being defrauded by further excesses committed with impunity [by this person] who has the appearance of a woman. This I do order and sign, I, the subdelegate of this region, acting with witnesses due to the absence of a scribe, which I do hereby certify.

Francino Valdés
José Manuel Rivas
Pio Rivas

In the town of Santa Ana, on the 28th of April, 1801. I, Don Domingo de Figueroa, First *Alcalde Ordinario* of this region, do say, that a woman who works as a peddler and is named Juana has been denounced as a man in disguise, and she presents herself this way to live with liberty, and in relations out of wedlock that she has with Catarina Pérez, a tributary *India* of the town of Cojutepeque, who keeps company with her. And to find out the truth and proceed to the punishment of these deeds, she must be identified by two matrons or midwives, and if necessary by the Surgeon Don Sebastián de Carranza, and the Professor of Medicine Don Josef Joaquín Ciliezar, while securing, of course, the aforementioned Juana and Catarina in the detention house to avoid their escape as mentioned in the documents, and all persons with knowledge of the mentioned crime should be questioned. This I do order and sign, with the stated witnesses due to the absence of a scribe.

Figueroa
Lorenzo Alvarado
Juan Saturnino Álvarez

On the same day, at ten in the evening, I, the *alcalde ordinario* by means of the *alcalde de barrio* Josef Felipe Santo, did order arrested the said Juana and Catarina Pérez, placing the first in the house of Juliana Cateja and the second in the house of Tomás Antonio Ayala, which is hereby affirmed by the signature of witnesses.

Figueroa
Lorenzo Alvarado
Juan Saturnino Álvarez

On the 29th of the said month and year I, the stated *alcalde ordinario,* made appear before me Juana Matías Morán, midwife by trade, who took the oath before the witnesses assisting me and in accordance with this oath promised to say the truth. She said, in accordance with the previous order I meticulously examined Juana, who by way of insult is called "*larga,*" and that this woman has a kind of uterus, but it is closed and smooth, and above it she has a small nib like the male member of a child, about the length of half a finger. And that is as much as she can say and it is the truth in accordance with her oath. Her deposition was read back to her and she said she cannot sign and is more than fifty years of age.

Figueroa
Lorenzo Alvarado
Juan Saturnino Álvarez

Subsequently, with the Surgeon Don Sebastián Carranza and Professor of Medicine Don Joaquín Ciliezar present, I, the aforementioned *alcalde ordinario,* took their oaths separately before the witnesses assisting me and having formalized their oaths they said the following: that having examined Juana *Larga* they found situated above the clitoris a small male member, small and very short with a loose foreskin, without an opening at the tip and without external testicles similar in size to that of a boy of six years of age. With regard to the cavity of the uterus, it goes no further than connecting the clitoris to where the fallopian tubes are formed, and the rest, which is closed by nature, continues to the edge of the anus, and only this defect is notable in the uterus, which examination demonstrates that this is a legitimate hermaphrodite. And this is as much as they can offer with their expertise; this is the truth in accordance with the oath that they have taken. The first said he was sixty-three years old and has practiced [medicine] for forty-six years and the second is fifty years old and has practiced for more than thirty. They signed with me and the witnesses who are assisting me due to the absence of a scribe.

Figueroa
Sebastián Carranza

Josef Joaquín de Ciliezar
Lorenzo Alvarado
Juan Saturnino Álvarez

On the same day, I, the said *alcalde ordinario*, ordered María del Rosario Aguilar to appear before me. She is native to San Salvador and is a resident in this town, and before witnesses she took the oath and promised to say the truth in all that was asked of her. Asked if she has knowledge of Juana María *Larga*, peddler by profession, she said that she had seen her for the first time some eight years ago in the town of Cojutepeque, and that there she heard, she doesn't remember from whom, that [Aguilar] was originally from León, and that in the said town [of Cojutepeque] she was accused of living out of wedlock with an *India* named Petrona Pérez who died in childbirth in Jutiapa, according to what she heard from Nasaria So-and-So,[13] who is employed in the house of Doña Nicolasa Quintana. She was put in jail for the crime by the Deputy Intendant Don Jacobo Núñez de Araujo, and because she was ill they detained her in the home of Doña Antonia Castillo, from which she escaped, and she [the declarant] has not seen her again until now that she found her accompanied by Catarina Pérez, sister of the said Petrona. [She said that] she is aware that the aforementioned Juana *Larga* is a male, and she knows this because in the said town she had once gone to keep her company at night and she [Juana] wished to have carnal relations with her, and that in the act of pulling away because she did not consent to going through with it she noticed that she [Juana] had a male member like men did, and that it was erect, and that afterwards she [Juana] began asking her to do the same dishonest act, offering to give her whatever she needed, but that she [the declarant] did not consent. That this is the truth by the oath she has taken, and once the deposition was read to her she affirmed it and signed it, stating that she was thirty-four years old.

Figueroa
Lorenzo Alvarado
Juan Saturnino Álvarez

Subsequently, I, the aforementioned *alcalde ordinario*, did order to appear before me Juana Nasara Jatero of Ahuechapán, currently

13. "De tal," the common expression for a name one cannot remember, as in "Fulano de tal."

resident of Metapas, and servant in the house of Doña Nicolasa Quintana, and before the witnesses I gave her the oath which she made in the name of God Our Lord and a sign of the cross, offering to tell the truth in all that she knew and was asked. Asked with regard to the event related in the prior testimony by María del Rosario Aguilar and in the principal case, she said that it is true that Petrona Pérez died in the town of Jutiapa. That about six years ago she met Juana *Larga* in the town of Esquipulas, and that afterwards she had seen her in various places with the motive of pursuing her profession as a peddler and that it is widely known[14] that [Aguilar] has both sexes and that one time out of curiosity she wished to see her in the river bathing but she wasn't able to. That at that time she saw her accompanied by an *India* from Cojutepeque named Petrona Pérez who, someone told her, she doesn't remember who, had died in Jutiapa in childbirth. That the said Petrona had sent for her sister, Catarina Pérez, to come to the said town and that the aforementioned Juana had commenced going around with her but [the declarant] doesn't know if [Aguilar] uses [Catarina] ill or not. That what she has said is the truth by the oath that she has given, and read her deposition she affirmed it and stated that she was thirty years old and did not sign because she could not. I did so before the witnesses.

Figueroa
Lorenzo Alvarado
Juan Saturnino Álvarez

Santa Ana, May 28, 1801

Due to what emerges in the declaration of María del Rosario Aguilar, about the creation of case files in the jurisdiction of the Deputy Intendant of Cojutepeque against Juana *Larga* for the crime described, let a letter be written to the official of the said town so that he will send, if convenient, the case initiated in his jurisdiction, so that it can be added to the one being assembled here.

Coubtiño
Lorenzo Alvarado
Juan Saturnino Álvarez

14. Here the word is *notorio*, a term that sounds similar to "notorious" but in the colonial period was used to mean something broadly known by the public.

It was sent on the same date.

Santa Ana, June 5, 1801

Let the case against Juana *Larga* in the documents sent by the Deputy Intendant of Cojutepeque be added to this file, and let notice be sent to Don José Tomás de Zelaya, Attorney of the Royal *Audiencia* of this Kingdom. This I do order and sign, Don Salvador de Coubtiño, Deputy Consular and First *Alcalde Ordinario* of this region, acting with witnesses due to the absence of a scribe.

Coubtiño
Lorenzo Alvarado
Juan Saturnino Álvarez

This case, due to its seriousness, its strangeness, the diversity of ideas it presents and the other singular circumstances that in it occur, is the kind that should be reviewed by the Superior [Court] in accordance with the doctrine of *Señor* Don Lorenzo Mateu, presented in his treatise *de re criminali* in the third controversy.[15]

The *asesor*[16] is well aware of the precedent established by the legal authority of Ulpian and Paulus, the first in the Laws, folio 10, *Statu o hominum* and [folio] 6 § 2.0 *de liveais et posthumis* and from the second, in Law 15 of § 1 *de testibus*.[17] He also has present the controversy #48 of the same *Señor* Mateu, in the cited treatise, and the doctrine of the celebrated medical legal scholar, Paulo Zaquias, in his work, *Quaestiones medico-legales*. Book 7, title 1, question 8.[18] De Carranza, in his work on *de parte naturali*,[19] chapter 17, no. 66, and

15. Here Zelaya refers to the Valencian jurist Lorenzo Mateu y Sanz (1618–1680), who directly addressed the problem of how hermaphrodites should be treated by the law in his work *Tractatus de re criminali*.

16. The *asesor* is Zelaya himself—either he has a scribe taking dictation or he writes about himself in the third person.

17. Zelaya is referring to the Roman jurists Ulpian and Paulus, who wrote about hermaphrodites in the legal context. See Gardner, "Sexing a Roman"; Kuefler, *Manly Eunuch*; Laes, Goodey, and Rose, *Disabilities in Roman Antiquity*.

18. Paolo Zacchia (1584–1659), a physician and medical-legal jurist who wrote on the nature of hermaphrodites in his three-volume work.

19. Alonso Carranza, the author of the 1628 work *Disputatio de vera humani partus naturalis et legitimi designationi*. See Cleminson and Vázquez García, *Hermaphroditism, Medical Science*, 46.

innumerable other theologians and jurists, unanimously agree upon the existence of certain monsters of this kind.

It is also understood that some modern critics, like Doctor Martín Martínez and the Abbot Hervás y Panduro, deny not only the reality or existence of them but also the very possibility of such creatures.[20]

The *asesor* has very little or no knowledge of physiology or anatomy, but nevertheless it is not lost on him that Juana Aguilar, alias *Larga,* might not rigorously or properly be a hermaphrodite and yet might appear to be one to those who have no idea of what vices and perfections nature creates.

What we really see in the trial documents of Cojutepeque, and in the town itself, is that Juana Aguilar has something above her natural female genitals: a certain excrescence or meatiness, in the mode of a penis or male member, of about an inch or two fingers' width in length, but without a urethra, or other channel for the ejection of semen, although capable of and susceptible to erection.

These tricks or venalities of nature often come about due to frequent or excessive use or exercise of carnal acts, and that is surely what was brought to light by Don Sebastián Carranza and Don Joaquín Ciliezar, as is evident by their depositions, and perhaps after all they have less knowledge of things relating to physiology than the *asesor*.

Be that as it may, what is in no doubt is that Juana *Larga* has abused the insinuated protuberance in a manner criminal, heinous, and punishable by seducing others and engaging in an execrable and ruinous congress with people of her same sex, whose vices, as the *asesor* understands it, can be cured by an able practitioner.

For this reason, it is ordered that Your Grace send these files and the corresponding case to the Royal Criminal Court, so that, if [the court] considers it expedient, Juana *Larga* be conducted to this capital, and the documents passed to the Protomedicato, or a study be made by intelligent experts, or it may resolve what is just, and in the meantime the aforementioned Juana will remain in custody, separated from men and women.

20. Here he references anatomist Martín Martínez (1684–1734) and Jesuit Lorenzo Hervás y Panduro (1735–1809), two scientific thinkers of the eighteenth century. Martínez's work *Complete Anatomy of Man* (1728) construed sex difference as a crucial element of social order. See Vicente, *Debating Sex and Gender*; Flores de la Flor, *Visión médica del monstruo*.

Guatemala, August 3, 1801
José Tomás de Zelaya

Santa Ana, August 10, 1801

As the *asesor* has directed that Juana Aguilar (alias *Larga*) should remain for now detained as she has been in the house of Juliana Cateja, with the goal of avoiding all communication with men and women, she shall be reminded of the responsibility of keeping her there so that she does not escape.

Coubtiño
José Tomás Samayoa
Juan Saturnino Álvarez

August 14, 1801

Juliana Cateja having reported that Juana Aguilar (alias *Larga*) has escaped from her house last night at about twelve, leaving the luggage that had contained her clothes full of stones, so that her absence would not be noticed. And since she should have remained in prison until the Royal Court could determine a just outcome, it is requested by the authorities of this jurisdiction, that the warrant be released far and wide with her description in order to apprehend her.

Coubtiño
José Tomás Samayoa
Juan Saturnino Álvarez

The orders and warrants were released on the same day.

Santa Ana, 13 of July, 1802

Having received notice on this day that Juana Aguilar (alias *Larga*) is in Guatemala, I hereby uphold what was ordered on August 10 of last year, accompanied by her description.

Coubtiño

An entry [of this case] is made in the record book.

José Tomás Samayoa
Juan Saturnino Álvarez

With the corresponding consultation, I hereby send to Your Grace the criminal case against Juana Aguilar (alias *Larga*) for the heinous criminal abuse that she has committed, soliciting and engaging in illicit friendship with people of the same sex, so that Your Grace may give account to the Royal Court and notify me of receipt.

God keep Your Grace for many years.

Santa Ana, 14 July, 1802.

Salvador de Coubtiño

[Addressed to: *Señor Secretario* Don Joaquin José Calvo]

[A small cover sheet for the letter:]

To Don Joaquín José Calvo, scribe of the royal civil court, who also serves the Royal Criminal Court of this Kingdom.

[Official mail stamp of Santa Ana:]

Office of the criminal court

New Guatemala[21]

Esteemed Sir,

The *alcalde ordinario* of the first instance in the state of Santa Ana, reports to Your Grace with the criminal case against Juana Aguilar (alias *Larga*) for the heinous criminal abuse that she has committed, soliciting and engaging in an execrable and punishable congress with people of the same sex, and who, on the verge of being sent last August 14, escaped from the prison in which she was held, and it was indispensable to undertake certain measures to recapture her, until it came to their notice that the said Juana Aguilar was in fact in this capital, plying her trade as a peddler, with a store that she has on the corner of the house of the Marquis of Aycinena and the street that goes toward the house of Don Tadeo Piñol, next to the stall of Cleta Alvarado, in the care of a young man of white face and low body who can offer information about her whereabouts. She is tall, with a normal body, and with an aspect more similar to men when they are dressed as women, without breasts. She speaks crudely and is fifty years of age more or less, with brunette, curly hair that has a crispy texture like that of the Blacks. She dresses well for her social station, and she uses a string of coral beads. Notice was given that she had parted from her accomplice, Catarina Pérez, who is accompanied by

21. This was the name still used, more than twenty-five years after its relocation, for what would become Guatemala City.

her consort Bruno Atiliano López (whom she married after fleeing said Aguilar) and another *indizuela* from the Province of Chiquimula, named María Candelaria López; they departed for that city in search of her. This is made known to Your Grace so that you may determine how to proceed in the name of Justice.

May Our Lord keep Your Grace's Catholic Royal Person many years. Santa Ana, July 14, 1802.

Most Illustrious Sir

Salvador de Coubtiño

The Royal Court, July 21, 1802

The *Alguacil Mayor* of the court is charged with the imprisonment of Juana Aguilar. Give notice to the court.

This was certified by the three officials noted here, which I do affirm,

Joaquín José Calvo

On the 29th of the same month and year, I, the *escribano*, make note that the Minister Manuel Quiroa, ordered by His Grace the *Alguacil Mayor* of the court, did place Juana Aguilar in prison and give my notice of the same, and His Grace ordered me to inventory her belongings, depositing them with Don Juan Campos, and placing her in the custody of the warden of the women's prison, which I do here attest was done, adding the list of embargoed belongings.

Ramón Arriaza

List of goods belonging to Juana Aguilar and deposited with Don Juan Campos, *Alcayde* of the Royal Court, and they are the following:

First, a trunk of old leather with its netting, containing a large cloth of thick thread
also: four dolls
also: nineteen images of San Antonio made of tin
also: one small reliquary of the same with water
also: seventy small pieces of yellow metal, such as crosses, rings, roosters, toothpicks
also: sixty-eight pieces of white metal, as above
also: one hundred twenty-nine rosaries made of strung beads
also: four St. Ignatius beans and two nutmegs

also: twenty-nine strung beads, multicolored, for the Paternoster
also: two gross and eight strung rosaries, multicolored
also: two gross and five dozen rosaries of the same [multicolored]
also: one pair of spectacles
also: silver earrings with pale blue false gems
also: five skeins of fine gold thread
also: a small trunk with a few colored silks

With which the list was concluded by the *Señor Alguacil* of the Court, without there being additional goods despite their being requested, and to verify this I do sign and the *alcalde* signs, noting receipt of everything listed above.
Juan Campos
Ramón Arriaza

I, the *escribano*, do affirm here that the prior list of goods of Juana Aguilar was made in the presence of His Grace the *Alguacil Mayor* and the warden of the women's prison, who acknowledged custody of the said Aguilar, and they sign here.
Barroeta
Ramón Arriaza

Very Esteemed Sir,
The Court Official reports to Your Grace with news of the imprisonment of Juana Aguilar (alias *Larga*), who has been placed in a cell in the women's prison with the necessary warnings to the warden.

The goods found on her person (with the exception of the few articles of clothing she was wearing) are those noted in the document above, which are deposited with the *Alcayde* of the court, Don Juan Campos, and at Your Grace's disposal. New Guatemala, August 13, 1802.
Very Esteemed Sir
Joseph Manuel de Barroeta

Royal Criminal Court, September 10, 1802
Having seen these documents, order was given to pass the case to the Protomedicato Doctor Don José Córdova so that Juana *Larga* may

be examined by the practitioners of his choosing, who under oath will offer a report of their findings, including any recommendations they may have for how the medical arts might remedy these vices of nature.

[In the margin:]

Judges Robledo, Collado

This was ordered and signed by the gentlemen in the margin, as I do affirm.

Joaquín José Calvo

Royal Tribunal of the Protomedicato of Guatemala, September 15, 1802

In order to fulfill the preceding orders of the Superior Court, received last night, the Doctors Don Narciso Esparragosa and Don José María Guerra will visit the women's prison to examine Juana Aguilar *Larga* and, under oath, will inform Your Grace about everything indicated in the stated document, and once completed it will be presented to the *escribano* so that he may give it to the office.

Doctor José Antonio Cordova

Before me, Josef Díaz Gonzales

On the said day I made it known to the Doctors Don Narciso Esparragosa and Don José María Guerra, and they acknowledged the orders. I gave them the documents, which they signed.

Díaz

Most Esteemed Sir,

To fulfill the orders in the preceding document, I went to the women's prison to conduct the examination of Juana Aguilar, the result of which I will offer under a binding oath. Beginning with the upper part of this woman's genitals, one can see the top of the labia, as in all women below the pubic bone. These open and descend to below the opening of the urinary tract, from which point they appear closed until they reach the branching point next to the anus. The clitoris, which occupies its natural spot, although it protrudes somewhat from the labia, is of a medium to large size, close to one inch in length, and thick as a little finger, of a medium density. As other women do, she has a foreskin, and the membranes that begin near what anatomists called the "ninfas" do descend in the usual way toward the urinary tract but are disfigured. The tract is located in the correct place, and probing it lightly it seems to be a little longer than usual and that it connects only to the bladder.

This is what we can observe externally of this woman's genitals, and it is all we have to characterize her sex, nature having left her without the use of the intended purpose of coitus and perhaps absolutely without [reproductive organs]. It is not easy to decide in which of these two states the unhappy person finds herself—that is, in the state of having only a closed vulva, but with a [concealed] vaginal canal that would serve for the introduction of a male member, or if in addition to having a closed vulva, she also lacks a vagina, because Mr. Levret,[22] the surgeon who belonged to the College of Paris, and the celebrated obstetrician of Madam Delphine, says: that women who find themselves with this cruel deformity may lack all or part of the vagina.

I detect these qualities in this woman, and I am inclined to believe that Levret's opinion would be realized in this case, were the vulva open, because when I asked her if she menstruated she replied that she did so through the urinary opening, with a blood like the runoff of meat. Asked if in the course of congress that she might have had with some man, she had felt pleasure and the effusion of semen, she answered that a few times it did occur that she joined with a man, although he did not have a place to penetrate, and she reverted to the same urinary opening, which argues conclusively for some kind of a connection between the neck of the uterus and the urinary tract, which can only be conceived of and explained by the absence of a vagina, because if it did exist, the blood and other fluid should run with greater facility toward it, as the channel with the steeper decline and greater diameter, than toward any other passage, longer and more tortured, which the communicating passage we have been discussing would be. This probable conjecture is corroborated by the opinion of Levret, and his finding that the woman [he examined] lacked a vaginal canal.

After these reflections, if we turn to the matter of remedies that the [surgical] arts can offer to correct the deformities of nature, I am convinced that if we practiced the operation that seems to be

22. André Levret (1703–1780), a renowned Parisian obstetrician.

indicated, we would find it ineffective, and I am even more inclined to think so when we consider that it would be practiced upon a woman who has already lived two-thirds of her life.

On the other hand, the accusation that is made against this woman in the case persuades me to speak once again of the size I have observed of the clitoris, which is not especially erect, nor is it robust enough for this woman to have committed the crime. And so, I am inclined to see this case of *nefando*[23] less as the result of an enlarged clitoris than as the result of the impossibility of cohabiting with a man, which has been the misfortune of this unhappy woman. Her ignorance makes her believe she is a hermaphrodite, the fame of which, popularly known, I am convinced, seduced other women into satisfying their curiosity with Aguilar, to see if it is true and to experiment the effects of a copulation that would otherwise be entirely lacking in pleasure for them, since certainly this woman's solicitations, without the reputation of a hermaphrodite, would be for other women entirely unappealing. And that is as much as I can offer on the matter. Guatemala, November 20, 1802

Very Illustrious Sir
Doctor José María Guerra

Ever since Mythology placed among her inventions the beauteous Hermaphrodite who, united with the Nymph *Salmacis*,[24] was converted into one identical person with two sexes, it seems as if the real and physical existence of that monster of nature was born.[25] Not only did it make its mark among the common people, who easily lend credulity to everything presented with an air of mystery and belonging to a sphere beyond the natural, but it also seized the imagination of some Philosophical Anatomists and Physicians, who ennobled that false phantom with accoutrements of proof, which they readily

23. *Nefando* here is shorthand for *pecado nefando*, or "heinous sin," which was synonymous with sodomy.

24. A naiad nymph of Greek mythology. As recounted in Ovid's *Metamorphosis*, Salmacis attempted to force herself upon Hermaphroditus, a beautiful young man who was the child of Aphrodite and Hermes. When Hermaphroditus rejected her, Salmacis begged the gods to let her stay with Hermaphroditus forever, and they responded by joining them together into a single body. This myth is the origin of the term "hermaphrodite."

25. This testimony by Esparragosa, beginning here and with some modifications, was published in the Guatemalan *Gazeta* in July 1803.

believed, dazzled by the prevalent public opinion; and that powerful current dragged along with it almost all of the philosophers of centuries past. By such good fortune the *androgenous* have occupied a very distinguished place among the beings of the universe, and since they present themselves as uncontested physical dogma, they have not only prompted sacred science to consider them as objects of discussion, but they have also found a place for themselves in the codices of the wisest legal thinkers. But experience protests, and two wise figures from the century that has just ended, the Count de Buffon and the Abbot Hervás, alone among a multitude of Physicians and Anatomists, argue against this monster with the unyielding laws of nature.[26] These two, whose profound knowledge [and] respectable authority [are] erected on the incontestable throne of observation and the most conclusive rationality, oblige me to follow in their footsteps, not having any positive proof that discredits their assertions. But despite the fact that this chimera has received a mortal blow, so that its existence only exists in the vast realm of imagination, there persists a popular opinion that is as willing to believe as it is difficult to correct.

And, of course, the present case of Juana *Larga*, object of my investigations in this report, would have been cited as proof positive, an irrefutable corroboration of Hermaphroditism in future ages, had it not been for how the criminal excesses imputed to her placed her at the mercy of Your Grace's Tribunal, which found the most prudent and precise means of unmasking this phenomenon, whose existence is taken to be proven and supported by the statements and repeated examinations herein. But the excited mind is so capable of error! And ignorance is capable of producing so many exaggerations! Juana *Larga* not only fails to join the two sexes: she lacks the proper male organs, *and* nature has also denied her what is necessary to make her a woman—a strange phenomenon! In demonstrating this truth to Your Grace, resulting from the most scrupulous and faithful observation, it is indispensable to describe in an abbreviated way the external sexual organs as they are seen in women by simple sight in their natural state. Then analyzing those belonging to Juana, we will realize by direct contrast the difference between one and the other,

26. Georges-Louis Leclerc, comte de Buffon (1707–1788), a French naturalist who was greatly influential among Latin American Enlightenment thinkers.

and the deformity of those [belonging to Aguilar] will make evident what is mere excess and what is defect.

The region below the belly that is covered with hair between the inner thighs, is popularly called the pubis or the groin; immediately below this there are two oblong protrusions, one beside the other, which descend to near the anus, bulkier in the front than in the back, and separated from top to bottom by a large fissure, and these parts have been baptized by the Anatomists with the name of "wings" or "lips": when opened, there is found between them in the upper part a small and somewhat prominent mass, very similar to the male member, called the clitoris, whose qualities make indispensable more detailed description, because it is the organ that plays in this case a very distinct and impressive role: its upper part and sides are covered with a kind of foreskin resulting from folds that occupy a position within the lips. These folds, as they descend toward the lower point and become wider for the opening of the vagina, form the vaginal lips: not only is the external shape of the clitoris very similar to a male member, but so is its internal structure, so that according to the universal agreement of the most celebrated Anatomists, only the absence of the urethra or the conduit from which the urine is ejected makes the difference between these organs in the two sexes. This has been demonstrated with the very precise illustrations of Regnier de Graaf, who after many dissections elaborated his excellent work on this topic.[27] The clitoris also has its internal muscles and its ligaments, as the male member does, and these elements make it capable of erection in like manner; the size of the clitoris varies, so that while it is usually not more than half an inch long it has also been too frequently observed to be of an extraordinary size, as several Surgeons and Anatomists have verified, such that among people of Egypt and in several oriental nations it is not uncommon to engage in a certain excess, finding it necessary for women to suffer a cauterization or amputation so that they will be suitable for marriage, and this kind of surgery is very common in those nations as much out of need as for decorum, according to the testimony of Belon.[28]

27. Dutch physician Regnier de Graaf (1641–1673), who contributed to early anatomists' conceptions of the human reproductive system, especially with regard to the fallopian tubes.

28. Esparragosa refers here to the French writer Pierre Belon (1517–1564), a writer and naturalist whose travels in the 1540s to Asia Minor, Egypt, and Arabia formed the basis for some of his writings.

The organ that I have just described, the Physiologists have conceded, has the capacity to excite concupiscence; because no other part [of the body] receives greater pleasure during coitus, it has been named by the anatomists *amoris dulcedo, oestrum veneris libidinis sedes.*[29] The indulgence in such liberties and the excessive swelling [of the clitoris] have contributed greatly to the reprehensible abuses committed by some Women who capriciously satiate their lust, defrauding what nature has granted to men, as was by turns admired and criticized elegantly by the poet Martial.[30]

The error of Hermaphroditism has resulted from the abovementioned excessive swelling, as the Comte de Buffon explains, because anatomists who are even more incautious than they are inexact during their dissections believed they were seeing the combination of the two sexes when it was really nothing more than the organs of a woman with an enlarged clitoris. This has been confirmed by the observations of Mr. Ferrein[31] and Regnier de Graaf.

Below the clitoris, between the lips, there is found a perforation that is the conduct for urine. And below this there is another quite large orifice that is the vagina, into which the male member is insinuated for the purposes of reproduction. I must make note of other circumstances relating to the externalities of female genitalia, which, although they have their uses destined by nature, do not for the moment require our attention.

I will go on now to report on what I have observed in the exterior sexual organs of Juana *la Larga*, and consequently I will demonstrate the reason for the error and the illusion that so many have been taken with, including those that made prior observations, before the case was directed to the tribunal of the Protomedicato.

At first sight, the lips of *la Juana* are observed to be large, the same as they would be on any woman, with the difference that the clitoris protrudes from them, a little more than half an inch, which is not very strange, since in some women a similar prominence is noted. Once the lips are separated, and the clitoris is observed from its base, it is evident that its length is about an inch and a half, in

29. Latin: the sweetness of love, or the "seat" of the libido. In medical dictionaries of the nineteenth century, the first phrase would be synonymous with the clitoris.

30. A Roman poet born in what is today Spain. His twelve books of epigrams, published between 86 and 103 CE, contain a lively commentary about the promiscuity of women.

31. Antoine Ferrein (1693–1769), a French anatomist.

thickness about that of a pinky or little finger on the hand of a man, its external shape perfectly similar to that of a male member, with its glans and foreskin. But it lacks the conduit for urine with which the male member is longitudinally perforated. The consistency of the clitoris is so flaccid that it falls by its own weight against the other parts, without noting in it even the slightest erection with different examinations and touches. Below this can be seen the vaginal lips, although they are somewhat wasted; the urinary opening can also be seen, although it is longer than usual, and this canal has served not only to excrete urine but also, as the same Juana has reported, for the discharge of a diluted menstruation. But the vaginal opening is entirely closed, or, more accurately, there is not even the slightest vestige of a vaginal orifice, which is that external organ most essential to women, since without it reproduction is impossible. And proceeding to examine whether the skin serves only to cover the vagina, so that if this were the case a convenient operation could be undertaken, to discover the opening, the reflection offered by Doctor Don Josef María Guerra in his preceding report seemed to me very judicious, in keeping with the findings of Mr. Levret, who assures us that women who find themselves with the external opening to the vagina covered up lack entirely the corresponding internal organs. This is exactly what I have observed in *la Juana*, because the body parts that find themselves below the skin in that region that should have the vagina are solid and firm, without any hint of an opening, and as a consequence this seems to militate against any operation or external opening, without permitting any other option for the [surgical] arts to reshape those organs.

But a rare and singular thing I have observed in the said Juana are the two glandular masses, oval in shape, each about the size of a grain of cacao, that are situated between the two large lips, on the upper part, and almost in front of the clitoris, which are possessed of an extreme sensitivity and attached to cord-like tissue that comes down through the inner thigh, giving passage to the spermatic vessels in men and to the round ligaments in women. Ultimately these glandular masses seem quite analogous, if not identical to, the testicles of men, and the spermatic vessels to which they are attached are not so different, except that they descend to the testicles much farther down [on other men], and a larger length of skin covers them, which is known commonly as the scrotum or sac.

This observation presents such a strange phenomenon, that only the surgical knife would be capable of discovering if in truth they are male testicles, or if by chance they are a certain organ called ovaries in women, that with the turmoil and confusion of their making, should have been placed within the belly but nature placed them in a different and inferior place, pulling them out through the rings or openings through which male testicles descend, in the final months prior to birth.

This manner of reasoning is not fanciful but rather quite in keeping with anatomical discoveries, and the similarities that have been observed in the reproductive organs of the two sexes, a similarity asserted by the Comte de Buffon, in the observation that while the sexual organs of men and women appear externally so different, they are in essence more or less developed versions of the same thing. This idea was adopted by the Ancients, and it was illustrated by the ingenious reflections of Mr. de Daubenton, based on the most recent observations in the prior ages.[32] If this is true, then we have no reason to doubt that the present case is effected by a mere trick of nature, which appears to bend its own laws, resulting in beings with such a mistaken sex, that to observers it appears a metamorphosis, and they are judged to be men or women or both, without being exactly one nor the other, similar to the neutrality found among certain bees. With regard to the supposed hermaphrodite Juana, I am convinced that it is a case of mistaken or neutral sex, and it is precisely the conclusion reached by Valmont de Bomare,[33] for in his dictionary of natural history he affirms that the subjects who qualify themselves with that title [of hermaphrodite], far from being both men and women, are not ordinarily one or the other, and these individuals owe their singular shape to nothing more than the mischief of nature, with which ordinary creation has been interrupted. That is, I say again, the case in which Juana finds herself, due to a certain obscure misplacement and confusion, her sexual organs were in a primitive state of development, resulting in a truly unfortunate person, who has been denied by nature organs of reproduction which

32. Louis Jean-Marie Daubenton (1716–1800), an anatomist and medical expert who was an associate of the comte de Buffon.

33. Jacques-Christophe Valmont de Bomare (1731–1807), a French naturalist and author of the six-volume *Dictionnaire raisonné universel d'histoire naturelle* (1764–68), which Esparragosa cites here.

each individual treasures because not only do they offer the greatest pleasure but they also offer that most singular satisfaction, which is preserving and perpetuating one's self in the form of descendants. And so, no matter how we consider the organs of *la Juana*, they are insufficient for these goals, and I do not mean reproduction but even a modest kind of pleasure. She is not even capable of the sexual act as a woman, according to the evidence of the observations presented here; nor is she capable of it as a man. Because what pleasure would she derive from the introduction of her clitoris, which is so small, thin, and flaccid? And even if we accept that in the act of sexual congress a certain erection might be possible, the pleasure gained would not go much further than the obscene rubbing that women engage in because she lacks the capacity for ejecting semen, and this being the most effective and determinant circumstance of deriving pleasure, it cannot be achieved, given that she lacks the conduits through which that liquor should come, whether we consider Juana as a man or as a woman. From all this Your Grace may have a more exact idea, if he considers it convenient to look upon the illustrations made by one of the better artists of this city, copied in the presence of the original, and which I have in my possession. They present intuitively a phenomenon of such rarity in nature, and their publication would dispel the falsehood that has been so widely believed.

Now that the sexual attributes of *la Juana* are revealed with scrupulous precision, it is clearly evident how much reduced are the criminal excesses described without basis as *nefando*. Because, being neither man nor woman, Juana cannot undertake a crime that necessarily requires the existence of one of the two sexes. And as a consequence, I see this case as one excluded from what existing laws have prescribed on the subject. And if we consider the effects to which our own nature inclines us, whose completion we are almost compelled toward, what would our supposed Hermaphrodite do upon reaching an age when the sensual passions enliven the weapons of her continuous and vehement combats? She would feel excited and bend toward the carnal act with almost irresistible impulses, following the caprices suggested by her exterior as a woman, and she would submit to the act as such, and finding nothing more than mortification and discomfort, as has already happened to her many times, as she herself confessed in good faith; she would abandon that mode, and would try by the other, although it would result in absolutely nothing. But even if this were so, and even if she had committed the excesses attributed to her in the accusation, there are many things that minimize her criminality with regard to *pecado nefando*. Having derived no satisfaction as a woman, [but] before giving up the act as entirely impossible, it would have been necessary to pursue her impulses. And feeling the vibrations that gave rise to the flame of lust, she would find the means of extinguishing that flame through the instrument that she wrongly believed was given to her by nature—by which I mean, that clitoris which is like a little member, and in which she would feel sexual urges, supposing this to be where nature has located sensuality, which of course would be more enlivened if it were to be perceived as a male member.

I have considered Juana's crime in its worst possible light. Is there anyone who can confirm what is stated here, that she engaged in the abominable *nefando*? If she is neither man nor woman, it would be a violent law indeed that would falsify her identity as one of these two sexes in order to consider her a criminal and apply punishment, and in this case I would dare to say that there is not a verified violation of the law but an arbitrary suspicion.

It would seem that I have violently overstepped the limits of what is allowed me in my medical role by adventurously offering these reflections in favor of Juana's cause and in vindication of such a fatal falsehood. But I have done nothing more than deduce, as a physician, a legitimate conclusion, faithful and natural, resulting from the most precise observations, which dispel all of those circumstances that have made her crime so monstrous. As a result, I see dissipated by the bright light of experience that murky twilight of fantasy and ignorance with which the declarations describing carnal acts consummated by a man and the reports made by the midwives and surgeons, believing and affirming her to be a hermaphrodite, were created. Such horrors have made it possible for this unfortunate to suffer a punishment similar to that of the Athenians and Romans, who, as a result of their ignorant superstition and their false philosophy, exiled supposed Hermaphrodites to a desert island because they believed them to be bad luck. But we find ourselves in a century of greater enlightenment, and we can scoff at such foolishness. And the case of Juana has had the good fortune of being judged by the wise and prudent Tribunal overseen by Your Grace, which has been wise enough to proceed in a manner that will illuminate this matter that has caused such extraordinary concern throughout the Kingdom, intriguing so many in society with its physical as well as with its moral and political elements. [The tribunal] will rip off the enigmatic veil of a matter that by its extravagant disguise has caused so much scandal and has kept so many in anticipation of the outcome. And this is as much as I consider it right to offer Your Grace, under the oath I have taken. In the town of Escuintla, February 3, 1803.

Very Illustrious Sir.

Narciso Esparragosa y Gallardo

Royal Criminal Court, February 19, 1803.

This should be reported to the *relator*, once it has been seen by the *fiscal*.

Joaquín José Calvo

Very Illustrious Sir.

His Majesty's *fiscal* says that Juana Aguilar, alias *Larga*, is more deserving of compassion than punishment. Although she has been thought a woman and a man at the same time, and has been processed through the trial with this in mind, in reality she is neither one nor the other, as the Doctors Don Joseph María Guerra and Don Narciso Esparragosa indicate in their respective reports. An individual with rationality, whom nature has by one of its rare occurrences denied both sexes, is likely to be unhappy for all the days of her life, given that she cannot count herself among men or among women.

The *fiscal* dispenses with the concerns of past centuries, even up until the last, which he considers gravely mistaken despite having been considered authoritative. Those fabulous ideas and imagined realities have now been banished with the greater knowledge that in our own time has been acquired through the work of anatomy. And with this certainty, it is accurate to believe that despite the evidence offered in the trial, not only has Aguilar not committed the crimes attributed to her but she has not even been capable of committing them, because she does not have the capacity to renew her existence by means of reproduction.

The most we can be sure of, as Dr. Esparragosa has explained, is that she has had some attempted encounters, be they as a man or as a woman, but these, even if they were deemed possible, would be sufficiently punished by the repeated imprisonments that she has suffered and that are likely sufficient to have been effectively corrective. The greater difficulty offered by the case is the danger of recidivism to which the said Juana remains at risk, especially as she dresses like a woman. But for this there is no remedy.

Were the situation otherwise, it would be suitable to destine her to live among the beasts, without human contact. But she is not to blame [for her condition] such that she be treated with such harshness, and it would be a punishment up to now unknown to us, which is not imposed even on the greatest criminals.

Because of these considerations, it seems to the *fiscal* that Your Grace would be well served to order that she be set free without charges; her confiscated goods should be returned, and she should be severely cautioned, so that in future she abstains from abusing either of her apparent sexes, which she should really already know she does not have. And should she require some additional assurance, so that she should not be imprisoned by the judges who have known the circumstances of this case, they should be given by this office or Your Grace will determine what is judged best. Guatemala, March 17, 1803.

Piloña[34]

Royal Criminal Court, March 22, 1803.

Notice should be given by the *relator*.

Joaquín José Calvo

Royal Criminal Court, April 19, 1803.

In light of this, it is ordered: Juana Aguilar shall be set free, her obligations having been met by the time she has spent in prison. She shall be admonished that in future she shall abstain from any and all dishonest acts. Order her to declare a place of residence that she chooses, because the *Alguacil Mayor* of the court and the corresponding judge will be attentive to her conduct. Release her belongings to her, and give her a certified copy of this ruling.

[In the margin]

Honorable Sirs, Judges Robledo and Villa Urrutia

[Signatures]

Cerdán, Robledo, Villa Urrutia

34. This is Diego Francisco Piloña y Ayala, discussed in the introduction.

This is ordered and signed by the gentlemen in the margin, as I do certify.

Joaquín José Calvo.

On the twentieth of this month the aforementioned orders were carried out with Juana Aguilar, who, having been informed of them, said: that for eleven years she has been in this city, and this is where she has her business established, and that with this in mind she wishes to be domiciled in this city.

Which I certify,
Ramón Arriaza

New Guatemala, April 20, 1803

His Grace the *Alguacil Mayor* of the court, Don Antonio Batres, having seen the preceding document says: that the prior document by His Grace does not require him to take the sworn residency declaration of Juana Aguilar, as she wishes to do, the documents are returned for further consideration. This I do order and sign, before me which I do certify.

Antonio Batres
Ramón Arriaza

Royal Criminal Court, April 22, 1803

Juana Aguilar will remain in this city, and the *Alguacil Mayor* who is setting her free will vigilantly keep an eye on her conduct.

[Rubrics]

This was reviewed, ordered, and signed by the gentlemen in the margin, as I do certify.

New Guatemala, April 28, 1803.

So that the orders made here shall take effect, the *alguaciles* of the royal court shall keep an eye on the conduct of Juana Aguilar, making a report of any incident.

Antonio Batres
Before me, Ramón Arriaza

In the same day I made it known to the officials who signed on the preceding document, and they acknowledged receipt.

[Signatures]
Ortiz, García, Lanioza,
Ramón Arriaza
Agustín Ruiz, Alonso

On May 10, a copy was made for the interested party.
Calvo

READING QUESTIONS

Below are some reading questions for your consideration. These questions are by no means exhaustive; there is much more to discuss in this case, and perhaps further questions will come to mind as you read. Nor are these questions meant to guide you toward a particular conclusion: they do not have "right" answers. Instead, they are meant to invite reflection and interpretation. These deliberately open-ended questions will ideally result in multiple persuasive replies.

1. Aguilar is assigned a defense attorney in this case—a *procurador.* What kind of legal defense does Aguilar make, and what defense does the *procurador* make on Aguilar's behalf? Does this strike you as an effective defense?
2. What kind of evidence do the various court officials seem to value in this inquiry? How do they treat witness testimony? What about expert testimony? Do they seem to consider all people similarly credible, or are some witnesses given greater weight?
3. How do the various medical experts who examine Aguilar come across? What do you notice about the tone, length, and argumentation of the testimony they offer? Are there any assumptions (or core beliefs) that you can identify in their testimony?
4. Several nonexperts give testimony in this case about their interactions with Aguilar. What do you notice about the testimony they offer? Considering each witness in turn, what do you think they are trying to achieve with their testimony?
5. María Mejía is one of the most important witnesses in the case, given that her testimony initiates the principal set of accusations. How do you interpret her testimony, and in particular her explanation for the sexual encounter between herself and Aguilar?

6. Aguilar testified with words—though clearly under duress—and also "testified" through actions. What do Aguilar's actions argue or convey, in contrast to or as a complement to the recorded words? You might consider not only the repeated escapes from prison but also choices of profession, clothing, and companionship.
7. Narciso Esparragosa offers a particularly celebratory take on the Enlightenment. According to him, what has the Enlightenment achieved, and how does it contrast with past ages? How does this depiction fit with other depictions (by contemporaries or by present-day scholars) of the global enlightenments?
8. Consider the inventories of seized goods. With the first, of Aguilar's belongings, what do you notice? What items are not present in this list? What material goods would Aguilar need that do not appear? With the second list, what do these items tell us about what colonial consumers valued? Why, do you think, would Aguilar consider it profitable to carry these items across long distances?
9. This case shines a light on how officials in this particular place and time understood the necessity of policing both sexual behavior and gender identity. How does this kind of policing operate in other places and times?
10. What other activities or behaviors do you notice are being policed through this criminal case?
11. To follow the suggestion of Susan Crane, what are you going to do with the knowledge of Aguilar's invasive physical exams? Does the knowledge invite (or require) any action in the present?

CHRONOLOGY

~1762		Juana Aguilar is born in Cacahuatique, San Salvador.
~1777		Juana Aguilar flees an apprenticeship in San Miguel, San Salvador, and travels to Cojutepeque, San Salvador.
1790		Don Francisco Rodríguez, Deputy Intendant, considers accusations against Juana Aguilar brought by Josefa Chapina. Aguilar is examined by an *Español* and a midwife.
1791		On the order of the Governor of Sensuntepeque, Aguilar is examined once again.
1792	September 17	Marcos Perdomo brings a complaint against Juana Aguilar to Don Jacobo Núñez y Araujo in Cojutepeque. Statements are taken from various witnesses.
	September 18	Petrona Pérez and Juana Aguilar are placed in custody. Aguilar's belongings are seized.
	September 19	Juana Aguilar is examined by the midwife Michaela Rivas.
	September 20	Petrona Pérez flees her place of detainment in Cojutepeque.
	November 26	A defense counsel is assigned to Juana Aguilar in Cojutepeque. Aguilar is questioned about the charges.
	December 19	Don Jacobo Núñez y Araujo orders a new confession to be taken from Juana Aguilar, and he orders a physical examination by Santiago Rosales and Tomasa de la Cruz. The examination is carried out.
	December 27	Juana Aguilar flees imprisonment in Cojutepeque, and Don Jacobo Núñez y Araujo orders law enforcement to pursue Aguilar.

1793–1801		Juana Aguilar works as a peddler based out of Guatemala City, traveling along a long-distance network between Guatemala and San Salvador.
1801	April 28	In Santa Ana, San Salvador, Juana Aguilar is detained along with Catarina Pérez, the sister of Petrona Pérez.
	April 29	Juana Aguilar is examined in Santa Ana by the midwife Juana Matías Morán and two physicians, Don Sebastián Carranza and Don Joaquín Ciliezar.
	June 5	The officials in Santa Ana contact the high court in Guatemala about the case of Juana Aguilar.
	August 3	José Tomás de Zelaya of the Guatemalan high court responds, asking the case to be transferred to his jurisdiction.
	August 13	Juana Aguilar escapes imprisonment in Santa Ana, San Salvador.
1802	July 13	Officials in Santa Ana learn that Juana Aguilar has been discovered in Guatemala City, and they send the case paperwork there.
	July 29	Juana Aguilar is placed in the women's prison in Guatemala City. Aguilar's belongings are confiscated.
	September 10	The case of Juana Aguilar is referred to the Protomedicato in Guatemala City.
	September 15	Don Narciso Esparragosa and Don José María Guerra, physicians in Guatemala City, are ordered by the Protomedicato to examine Aguilar.
	November 20	Don José María Guerra offers his report on his physical examination of Aguilar.
1803	February 3	Don Narciso Esparragosa offers his report on his physical examination of Aguilar.
	March 17	Don Diego Francisco Piloña y Ayala of the Guatemalan *audiencia* reaches a verdict in the case of Juana Aguilar.
	April	Juana Aguilar declares residence in Guatemala City and is freed from prison.

GLOSSARY

alcalde de barrio: A law enforcement official, similar to a magistrate, charged with patrolling a particular neighborhood.

alcalde ordinario: A law enforcement official, similar to a magistrate, responsible for the administration of justice in a given city, like Santa Ana or Guatemala City.

alcayde: A bailiff or jailer.

alguacil: An official charged with fulfilling the directives of a court. In larger cities, there would be an *alguacil mayor,* or chief official of this kind, to supervise others.

asesor: A legal advisor, in this case to the *audiencia* of Guatemala City.

audiencia: A high court in major Spanish American cities that processed criminal and civil proceedings and also fulfilled an administrative function by effecting policy.

cabildo: A governance structure in Spanish American cities that functioned like a city council.

calidad: A colonial term for the mixed attributes of race and social status. Common terms to describe *calidad* include *India/Indio* (Indian), *negra/negro* (Black), *mestiza/mestizo* (mixed Indian and Spanish), *mulata/mulato* (mixed Black and Spanish), and *Española/Español* (Spanish). All of these terms are misnomers to some degree. For example, *Español* was less a designation of geographic origin than a description of high status and social whiteness; many people labeled *Español* were born in the Americas.

concubinato: The crime of having a relationship out of wedlock. *Concubinato* could be prosecuted in the secular court during the colonial period.

Don/Doña: A title designating high social standing; in this period, a title almost exclusively applied to people identified racially as *Español.*

escribano: An official scribe for a court or other official body.

fiscal: An attorney for the crown who acted as both prosecutor of criminal cases and manager of cases, recommending verdicts.

india/o: A legal category used to designate Indigenous Americans in the early colonial period that was also used throughout the period as a racialized term.

maestro: A title given for "mastery" in a given subject, such as surgery.

peso: A unit of currency, in silver; one *peso* was worth eight *reales*.

Protomedicato: The judicial and administrative office tasked with regulating the medical profession and matters relating to public health.

real: Along with the *peso*, a unit of currency; eight *reales* were worth one *peso*.

relator: An official for the court who prepared case summaries and reported proceedings from one official to another.

BIBLIOGRAPHY

Abad, Miguel Pino. *La pena de confiscación de bienes en el derecho histórico español*. Editorial Dykinson, 2014.

Abdelnur, Heather Judge. "A History of Highland Guatemalan Textiles: Lost Opportunities and Colonial Legacies, 1760–1820." PhD diss., Texas Christian University, 2005.

Avendaño, Xiomara. "Una reforma incompleta: La intendencia de San Salvador durante la crisis monárquica." *Diálogos: Revista electrónica de historia*, 2008, 3994–4008.

Barahona, Renato. *Sex Crimes, Honour, and the Law in Early Modern Spain: Vizcaya, 1528–1735*. Toronto: University of Toronto Press, 2003.

Barnes, Thomas C., Thomas H. Naylor, and Charles W. Polzer. "The Structure of Colonial Government." In *Northern New Spain: A Research Guide*. University of Arizona Press, 1981. Accessed May 8, 2024. https://open.uapress.arizona.edu/read/northern-new-spain-a-research-guide/section/d972097b-7255-4487-afe7-3140f71195eb.

Beck, Lauren, and Alena Robin. "Latin American Art, Visual and Material Culture in the Long Eighteenth Century: An Introduction." *Arts* 10, no. 4 (2021): 76.

Behrend-Martínez, Edward. "Making Sense of the History of Sex and Gender in Early Modern Spain." *History Compass* 7, no. 5 (2009): 1303–16.

———. "Manhood and the Neutered Body in Early Modern Spain." *Journal of Social History* 38, no. 4 (2005): 1073–93.

Berco, Cristian. "Producing Patriarchy: Male Sodomy and Gender in Early Modern Spain." *Journal of the History of Sexuality* 17, no. 3 (2008): 351–76.

Black, Chad Thomas. "Prosecuting Female-Female Sex in Bourbon Quito." In *Sexuality and the Unnatural in Colonial Latin America*, edited by Zeb Tortorici, 120–40. University of California Press, 2016.

Black, Georgina Dopico. *Perfect Wives, Other Women: Adultery and Inquisition in Early Modern Spain*. Duke University Press, 2001.

Bush-Turner, Kera. "Trans-Formative Motivations: The Reconstructed Identity of Catalina De Erauso." MA thesis, State University of New York at Buffalo, 2022.

Butler, Judith. *Gender Trouble: Tenth Anniversary Edition*. 2nd ed. Routledge, 1999.

Cadden, Joan. *The Meanings of Sex Difference in the Middle Ages: Medicine, Science, and Culture*. Cambridge University Press, 1995.

Castellón Osegueda, José Ricardo. "Hacienda, familia, movilidad geográfica y social en el actual El Salvador al final de la era colonial." *Revista de ciencias sociales y humanidades* 1, no. 1 (2022): 35–65.

Caswell, Michelle. "Khmer Rouge Archives: Accountability, Truth, and Memory in Cambodia." *Archival Science* 10, no. 1 (2010): 25–44.

Cleminson, Richard, and Francisco Vázquez García. *Hermaphroditism, Medical Science and Sexual Identity in Spain, 1850–1960*. University of Wales Press, 2009.

Crane, Susan A. "Choosing Not to Look: Representation, Repatriation, and Holocaust Atrocity Photography." *History and Theory* 47, no. 3 (2008): 309–30.

Daston, Lorraine, and Katharine Park. "The Hermaphrodite and the Orders of Nature: Sexual Ambiguity in Early Modern France." In *Premodern Sexualities*, edited by Louise Fradenburg and Carla Freccero, 117–36. Routledge, 1996.

Deans-Smith, Susan. "The Money Plant: The Royal Tobacco Monopoly of New Spain, 1765–1821." In *The Economies of Mexico and Peru During the Late Colonial Period, 1760–1810*, edited by Nils Jacobsen and Hans-Jürgen Puhle, 361–87. Colloquium Verlag, 1986.

De Erauso, Catalina. *Lieutenant Nun: The True Story of a Cross-Dressing, Transatlantic Adventurer Who Escaped from a Spanish Convent in 1599 and Lived as a Man*. Beacon Press, 1997.

Del Carpio Penagos, Carlos Uriel. "Producción y comercio de tabaco en Centroamérica a fines del período colonial." *LiminaR: Estudios sociales y humanísticos* 12, no. 2 (2014): 195–208.

Dinan, Susan E., and Debra Meyers. *Women and Religion in Old and New Worlds*. Routledge, 2001.

Dreger, Alice Domurat. "Hermaphrodites and the Medical Invention of Sex." In *Hermaphrodites and the Medical Invention of Sex*. Harvard University Press, 2009.

DuPlessis, Robert. *The Material Atlantic: Clothing, Commerce, and Colonization in the Atlantic World, 1650–1800*. Cambridge University Press, 2016.

Dyer, Abigail. "Heresy and Dishonor: Sexual Crimes Before the Courts of Early Modern Spain." PhD diss., Columbia University, 2000.

Earle, Rebecca. "Luxury, Clothing and Race in Colonial Spanish America." In *Luxury in the Eighteenth Century: Debates, Desires and Delectable Goods*, edited by Maxine Berg and Elizabeth Eger, 219–27. Palgrave Macmillan UK, 2003.

———. "Race, Clothing and Identity: Sumptuary Laws in Colonial Spanish America." In *The Right to Dress: Sumptuary Laws in a Global*

Perspective, c.1200–1800, edited by Giorgio Riello and Ulinka Rublack, 325–45. Cambridge University Press, 2019.

Erbig, Jeffrey. "Afterlives in Captivity: Indigeneity and Penal Deportation in Southeastern South America." *Atlantic Studies* 21, no. 3 (2024): 394–418.

Esparragosa, Doctor Don Narciso. "Hermafroditas." *Gazeta de Guatemala* 7, no. 310 (July 4, 1803): 269–72.

Fausto-Sterling, Anne. *Sexing the Body: Gender Politics and the Construction of Sexuality*. Basic Books, 2020.

Fernandez de Pinedo, Nadia, and Corinne Thépaut-Cabasset. "Memoirs of the Fruits of Globalization: The Markets for Chinese Textiles in New Spain by Jean de Monségur." In *The Fruits of the Early Globalization: An Iberian Perspective*, edited by Rafael Dobado-González and Alfredo García-Hiernaux, 261–306. Springer, 2021.

Few, Martha. *For All of Humanity: Mesoamerican and Colonial Medicine in Enlightenment Guatemala*. University of Arizona Press, 2015.

———. "'That Monster of Nature': Gender, Sexuality, and the Medicalization of a 'Hermaphrodite' in Late Colonial Guatemala." *Ethnohistory* 54, no. 1 (2007): 159–76.

Flores de la Flor, Maria Alejandra. "La visión médica del monstruo en la España moderna." In *Comercio y cultura en la edad moderna*, edited by Juan José Iglesias Rodríguez, Rafael M. Pérez García, and Manuel F. Fernández Chaves, 2697–709. Universidad de Sevilla, 2015.

Foucault, Michel. *The Birth of the Clinic*. Routledge, 2002.

Francois, Marie. "Cloth and Silver: Pawning and Material Life in Mexico City at the Turn of the Nineteenth Century." *The Americas* 60, no. 3 (2004): 325–62.

Gardner, Jane F. "Sexing a Roman: Imperfect Men in Roman Law." In *When Men Were Men*, edited by Lin Foxhall and John Salmon, 136–52. Routledge, 1999.

Gauderman, Kimberly. *Women's Lives in Colonial Quito: Gender, Law, and Economy in Spanish America*. University of Texas Press, 2003.

Goldmark, Matthew. "Reading Habits: Catalina de Erauso and the Subjects of Early Modern Spanish Gender and Sexuality." *Colonial Latin American Review* 24, no. 2 (2015): 215–35.

Guatemala. "Criminales contra Juana Aguilar (alias Larga)" (Criminal case against Juana Aguilar). 1803. Signatura A1, Legajo 4376, Expediente 35664. Archivo General de Centroamérica, Guatemala.

———. "Sobre establecimiento de casa de recogidas en San Salvador." 1799. Signatura A1, Legajo 4669, Expediente 40058. Archivo General de Centroamérica, Guatemala.

Herrera Mena, Sajid Alfredo. *El ejercicio de gobernar: Del cabildo borbónico al ayuntamiento liberal: El Salvador colonial, 1750–1821*. Publicacions de la Universitat Jaume I, 2013.

Heyam, Kit. *Before We Were Trans: A New History of Gender*. Seal Press, 2022.

Imada, Adria L. *An Archive of Skin, an Archive of Kin: Disability and Life-Making During Medical Incarceration*. University of California Press, 2022.

Johnson, Lyman L. *The Problem of Order in Changing Societies: Essays on Crime and Policing in Argentina and Uruguay*. University of New Mexico Press, 1990.

Johnston Aguilar, René. "De la casa de doncellas a la cárcel de mujeres: Sexualidad y disciplinamiento en Santiago de Guatemala durante el período colonial." *El taller de la historia* 9, no. 9 (2017): 12–27.

King, Helen. *The One-Sex Body on Trial: The Classical and Early Modern Evidence*. Routledge, 2016.

Komisaruk, Catherine. *Labor and Love in Guatemala: The Eve of Independence*. Stanford University Press, 2013.

Kuefler, Mathew. *The Manly Eunuch: Masculinity, Gender Ambiguity, and Christian Ideology in Late Antiquity*. University of Chicago Press, 2001.

Laes, Christian, Chris Goodey, and M. Lynn Rose. *Disabilities in Roman Antiquity: Disparate Bodies A Capite ad Calcem*. Brill, 2013.

LaFleur, Greta. *The Natural History of Sexuality in Early America*. Johns Hopkins University Press, 2018.

LaFleur, Greta, Masha Raskolnikov, and Anna Kłosowska, eds. *Trans Historical: Gender Plurality Before the Modern*. Cornell University Press, 2021.

Lauria-Santiago, Aldo. *An Agrarian Republic: Commercial Agriculture and the Politics of Peasant Communities in El Salvador, 1823–1914*. University of Pittsburgh Press, 1999.

Lavenia, Vincenzo. "Contaminating Infidels, Burnt Bodies, and Saved Souls: Sodomy and Catholicism in the Early Modern Age." In *Bodies in Early Modern Religious Dissent*, edited by Elisabeth Fischer and Xenia von Tippelskirch, 155–73. Routledge, 2021.

Lavrin, Asunción. *Sexuality and Marriage in Colonial Latin America*. University of Nebraska Press, 1992.

Lokken, Paul. "Transforming Mulatto Identity in Colonial Guatemala and El Salvador, 1670–1720." *Transforming Anthropology* 12, nos. 1–2 (2004): 9–20.

MacLachlan, Colin M. *Criminal Justice in Eighteenth-Century Mexico: A Study of the Tribunal of Acordada*. University of California Press, 2021.

Mancall, Peter C., and Daniela Bleichmar, eds. *Collecting Across Cultures: Material Exchanges in the Early Modern Atlantic World*. University of Pennsylvania Press, 2011.

Marshall, Daniel, and Zeb Tortorici, eds. *Turning Archival: The Life of the Historical in Queer Studies*. Radical Perspectives. Duke University Press, 2022.

Martínez, María Elena. "Archives, Bodies, and Imagination: The Case of Juana Aguilar and Queer Approaches to History, Sexuality, and Politics." *Radical History Review* 2014, no. 120 (2014): 159–82.

Martínez Ruiz, Enrique. *Policías y proscritos: Estado, militarismo y seguridad en la España Borbónica (1700–1870)*. Editorial ACTAS, 2014.

Mason, Rebecca M. "Medicine, Gender and Sex in Early Modern Spain: Eleno/a de Céspedes and the One-Sex Model." *eHumanista: Journal of Iberian Studies* 37 (2017): 357–69.

———. "Mutable Sex, Cross-Dressing, and the Mujer Varonil: Understanding Non-Normative Sex in Early Modern Spain." PhD diss., Ohio State University, 2016.

Mateu y Sanz, Lorenzo. *DD Laurentii Matthaeu et Sanz. Tractatus de Re Criminali Siue Controversiarum usufrequentium in causis criminalibus"* Lugduni: sumptibus Petri Bruyset & Sociorum, 1738. Accessed March 4, 2024. http://hdl.handle.net/11169/21029.

Matthew, Laura E. *Memories of Conquest: Becoming Mexicano in Colonial Guatemala*. University of North Carolina Press, 2012.

———. "Two Bigamists in Tehuantepec: Global(ized) Itineraries in Southern Mesoamerica, circa 1600." *Hispanic American Historical Review* 103, no. 2 (2023): 251–82.

McClive, Cathy. "Masculinity on Trial: Penises, Hermaphrodites and the Uncertain Male Body in Early Modern France." *History Workshop Journal* 68, no. 1 (2009): 45–68.

Méndez Zárate, Armando. "Ferias comerciales en Guatemala y El Salvador vistas por la prensa del siglo XIX." *Revista pueblos y fronteras digital* 17 (2022).

Mendieta, Eva. *In Search of Catalina de Erauso: The National and Sexual Identity of the Lieutenant Nun*. Center for Basque Studies, University of Nevada, Reno, 2009.

Mirow, Matthew Campbell. *Latin American Law: A History of Private Law and Institutions in Spanish America*. University of Texas Press, 2004.

Molina, Fernanda. "Sodomy, Gender, and Identity in the Viceroyalty of Peru." In *Sexuality and the Unnatural in Colonial Latin America*, edited by Zeb Tortorici, 141–61. University of California Press, 2016.

Odumosu, Temi. "The Crying Child: On Colonial Archives, Digitization, and Ethics of Care in the Cultural Commons." *Current Anthropology* 61, no. S22 (2020): S289–302.

Office of the High Commissioner of Human Rights. "Intersex People: OHCHR and the Human Rights of LGBTI People." Accessed May 10, 2024. https://www.ohchr.org/en/sexual-orientation-and-gender-identity/intersex-people.

Onetto Pavez, Mauricio. "Reflexiones en torno a la construcción de esferas de control y sensibilidades: Las casas de Recogidas, siglos XVI–XVIII." *Estudios humanísticos: Historia*, no. 8 (2009): 177–204.

Patch, Robert W. *Indians and the Political Economy of Colonial Central America, 1670–1810*. University of Oklahoma Press, 2013.

Pérez Fabregat, Clara. "El proceso de construcción del Estado de El Salvador: Una mirada desde el Oriente, 1780–1865." Thesis, Universitat de Barcelona, 2015.

Pérez-Villanueva, Sonia. *The Life of Catalina de Erauso, the Lieutenant Nun: An Early Modern Autobiography*. Rowman & Littlefield, 2014.

Perry, Mary Elizabeth. "The 'Nefarious Sin' in Early Modern Seville." *Journal of Homosexuality* 16, nos. 1–2 (1989): 67–90.

Phipps, Elena. "New Textiles in a New World: 18th Century Textile Samples from the Viceregal Americas." In *Textile Society of America 2014 Biennial Symposium Proceedings: New Directions; Examining the Past, Creating the Future*. Los Angeles, California, September 10–14, 2014. http://digitalcommons.unl.edu/tsaconf/898.

Pierce, Donna. "Popular and Prevalent: Asian Trade Goods in Northern New Spain, 1590–1850." *Colonial Latin American Review* 25, no. 1 (2016): 77–97. https://doi.org/10.1080/10609164.2016.1180786.

———. "Unpacking a Colonial Bride: The 1721 Dowry of Luisa Gómez Del Castillo of Santa Cruz de La Cañada, New Mexico." Edited by Emily J. Brown, Matthew J. Barbour, and Genevieve N. Head. *Papers of the Archaeological Society of New Mexico* 45 (2019): 181–95.

Porter, Amy M. "Las Bexareñas and Their Wills: Women's Material Culture and Cataloguing Practices in Spanish San Fernando de Béxar." In *Women, Collecting, and Cultures Beyond Europe*, edited by Arlene Leis, 202–10. Routledge, 2022.

Ramírez, Paul. *Enlightened Immunity: Mexico's Experiments with Disease Prevention in the Age of Reason*. Stanford University Press, 2018.

Real Academia Española. "Achimero." Tesoro de los diccionarios históricos de la lengua Española. Accessed May 15, 2024. https://www.rae.es/tdhle/achimero.

———. "Diego Francisco Piloña y Ayala." Historia Hispánica. Accessed May 28, 2024. https://historia-hispanica.rah.es/biografias/36905-diego-francisco-pilona-y-ayala.

Reis, Elizabeth. *American Sexual Histories*. 2nd ed. Blackwell Readers in American Social and Cultural History. Wiley-Blackwell, 2012.

———. *Bodies in Doubt: An American History of Intersex*. Johns Hopkins University Press, 2009.

Rex, Cathy. "Ungendering Empire: Catalina De Erauso and the Performance of Masculinity." In *Women's Narratives of the Early Americas and the Formation of Empire*, edited by Mary McAleer Balkun and Susan C. Imbarrato, 33–46. Palgrave Macmillan US, 2016.

Riello, Giorgio, and Prasannan Parthasarathi, eds. *The Spinning World: A Global History of Cotton Textiles, 1200–1850*. Oxford University Press, 2011.

Rodríguez-Alegría, Enrique. *How to Make a New Spain: The Material Worlds of Colonial Mexico City*. Oxford University Press, 2023.

Sellers-García, Sylvia. *Distance and Documents at the Spanish Empire's Periphery*. Stanford University Press, 2013.

———. "Walking While Indian, Walking While Black: Policing in a Colonial City." *American Historical Review* 126, no. 2 (2021): 455–80.

———. *The Woman on the Windowsill: A Tale of Mystery in Several Parts.* Yale University Press, 2020.

Skeehan, Danielle C. *The Fabric of Empire: Material and Literary Cultures of the Global Atlantic, 1650–1850.* Studies in Early American Economy and Society from the Library Company of Philadelphia. Johns Hopkins University Press, 2020.

Slater, John, María Luz López Terrada, and José Pardo Tomás, eds. *Medical Cultures of the Early Modern Spanish Empire.* New Hispanisms: Cultural and Literary Studies. Ashgate, 2014.

Solórzano F., Juan Carlos. "Haciendas, ladinos y explotacion colonial: Guatemala, El Salvador y Chiapas en el siglo XVIII." *Anuario de estudios centroamericanos* 10 (1984): 95–123.

Stein, Stanley J. "Tending the Store: Trade and Silver at the Real de Huautla, 1778–1781." *Hispanic American Historical Review* 77, no. 3 (1997): 377–407.

Stoler, Ann. "Colonial Archives and the Arts of Governance." *Archival Science* 2, no. 1 (2002): 87–109.

Stone, Abigail. "Finding Women in Their Lost Possessions: Personal Artifacts at the Luna Settlement." MA thesis, University of West Florida, 2023.

Subotić, Jelena. "Ethics of Archival Research on Political Violence." *Journal of Peace Research* 58, no. 3 (2021): 342–54.

Tortorici, Zeb, ed. *Sexuality and the Unnatural in Colonial Latin America.* University of California Press, 2016.

Trouillot, Michel-Rolph. *Silencing the Past: Power and the Production of History.* Beacon Press, 2015.

Vázquez García, Francisco, and Richard Cleminson. "El destierro de lo maravilloso: Hermafroditas y mutantes sexuales en la España de la Ilustración." *Asclepio: Revista de historia de la medicina y de la ciencia* 63, no. 1 (2011): 7–38.

Velasco, Sherry. "'If These Beds Could Talk': Narrating Lesbian Sex Acts in Early Modern Spain." *Revista canadiense de estudios hispánicos* 35, no. 1 (2010): 229–42.

Vicente, Marta V. *Debating Sex and Gender in Eighteenth-Century Spain.* Cambridge University Press, 2017.

Viquera Albán, Juan Pedro. *Propriety and Permissiveness in Bourbon Mexico.* Scholarly Resources, 1999.

Voekel, Pamela. "Peeing on the Palace: Bodily Resistance to Bourbon Reforms in Mexico City." *Journal of Historical Sociology* 5, no. 2 (1992): 183–208.

Vollendorf, Lisa. "Good Sex, Bad Sex: Women and Intimacy in Early Modern Spain." *Hispania* 87, no. 1 (2004): 1–12.

———. *The Lives of Women: A New History of Inquisitional Spain.* Vanderbilt University Press, 2005.

Wortman, Miles L. *Government and Society in Central America, 1680–1840.* Columbia University Press, 1982.

Wunder, Amanda. "Spanish Fashion and Sumptuary Legislation from the Thirteenth to the Eighteenth Century." In *The Right to Dress: Sumptuary Laws in a Global Perspective, c.1200–1800*, edited by Giorgio Riello and Ulinka Rublack, 243–72. Cambridge University Press, 2019.

Zepeda, Nora. "Perfecting the Woman's Body in Early Modern Spain." *Mester* 34, no. 1 (2005): 183–200.

INDEX

Maps and tables are indicated by italic page numbers. Notes are indicated by "n" followed by the note number.

latin american originals

Series Editor | Matthew Restall

This series features primary-source texts on colonial and nineteenth-century Latin America, translated into English, in slim, accessible, affordable editions that also make scholarly contributions. Most of these sources are published here in English for the first time and represent an alternative to the traditional texts on early Latin America. The initial focus of the series was on the conquest period in sixteenth-century Spanish America, but its scope now includes later centuries and aims to be hemispheric. LAO volumes feature archival documents and printed sources originally in Spanish, Portuguese, Italian, Latin, Nahuatl, Maya, and other Native American languages. The contributing authors are historians, anthropologists, art historians, geographers, and scholars of literature.

Matthew Restall is Edwin Erle Sparks Professor of Latin American History and Anthropology and Director of Latin American Studies at the Pennsylvania State University. He edited *Ethnohistory* for a decade and now coedits the *Hispanic American Historical Review*.

Titles in Print

Invading Colombia: Spanish Accounts of the Gonzalo Jiménez de Quesada Expedition of Conquest (LAO 1)
J. Michael Francis

Invading Guatemala: Spanish, Nahua, and Maya Accounts of the Conquest Wars (LAO 2)
Matthew Restall and Florine G. L. Asselbergs

The Conquest on Trial: Carvajal's "Complaint of the Indians in the Court of Death" (LAO 3)
Carlos A. Jáuregui

Defending the Conquest: Bernardo de Vargas Machuca's "Defense and Discourse of the Western Conquests" (LAO 4)
Edited by Kris Lane and translated by Timothy F. Johnson

Forgotten Franciscans: Works from an Inquisitional Theorist, a Heretic, and an Inquisitional Deputy (LAO 5)
Martin Austin Nesvig

Gods of the Andes: An Early Jesuit Account of Inca Religion and Andean Christianity (LAO 6)
Sabine Hyland

Of Cannibals and Kings: Primal Anthropology in the Americas (LAO 7)
Neil L. Whitehead

Translated Christianities: Nahuatl and Maya Religious Texts (LAO 8)
Mark Z. Christensen

The Improbable Conquest: Sixteenth-Century Letters from the Río de la Plata (LAO 9)
Pablo García Loaeza and Victoria L. Garrett

The Native Conquistador: Alva Ixtlilxochitl's Account of the Conquest of New Spain (LAO 10)
Edited and translated by Amber Brian, Bradley Benton, and Pablo García Loaeza

The History of the New World: Benzoni's "Historia del Mondo Nuovo" (LAO 11)
Translated by Jana Byars and edited by Robert C. Schwaller and Jana Byars

Contesting Conquest: Indigenous Perspectives on the Spanish Occupation of Nueva Galicia (LAO 12)
Ida Altman

To Heaven or to Hell: Bartolomé de Las Casas's "Confesionario" (LAO 13)
David Thomas Orique, O.P.

To the Shores of Chile: The "Journal and History" of the Brouwer Expedition to Valdivia in 1643 (LAO 14)
Mark Meuwese

Baptism Through Incision: The Postmortem Cesarean Operation in the Spanish Empire (LAO 15)
Martha Few, Zeb Tortorici, and Adam Warren, translated by Nina M. Scott

Indigenous Life After the Conquest: The De la Cruz Family Papers of Colonial Mexico (LAO 16)
Caterina Pizzigoni and Camilla Townsend

An Irish Rebel in New Spain (LAO 17)
Andrea Martínez Baracs

Pandemic in Potosí: Fear, Loathing, and Public Piety in a Colonial Mining Metropolis (LAO 18)
Kris Lane

Violent First Contact in Venezuela: Nikolaus Federmann's "Indian History" (LAO 19)
Peter Hess